The Probability of Fortune

The Probability of Fortune

Financial Strategies with the Best Odds

Moshe A. Milevsky, Ph.D.
with Michael Posner

Stoddart

Published in 2000 by Stoddart Publishing Co. Limited
180 Varick Street, 9th Floor, New York, New York 10014

Distributed in the United States by:
General Distribution Services Inc.
PMB 128, 4500 Witmer Industrial Estates
Niagara Falls, New York 14305-1386
Toll-free Tel. 1-800-805-1083 Toll-free Fax 1-800-481-6207
Email gdsinc@genpub.com

04 03 02 01 00 1 2 3 4 5

U.S. Cataloging-in-Publication Data
(Library of Congress Standards)

Milevsky, Moshe A.
The probability of fortune / Moshe A. Milevsky — 1st ed.
[208]p.: cm.

Summary: Aspects of personal investing, including investment protection, portfolio insurance options, dollar-cost averaging, lump-sum investing, etc.

ISBN 0-7737-3260-8

1. Investments. 2. Finance, Personal. I. Title.
332.024 21 2000 CIP

Jacket Design: Bill Douglas @ The Bang
Text Design and Typesetting: Kinetics Design & Illustration

The Canada Council for the Arts since 1957 | Le Conseil des Arts du Canada depuis 1957

We acknowledge for their financial support of our publishing program the Canada Council, the Ontario Arts Council, and the Government of Canada through the Book Publishing Industry Development Program (BPIDP).

Printed and bound in Canada

To my wife, Edna Ida

CONTENTS

	Acknowledgments	*ix*
	Introduction: What Are the Odds?	1
1	Your Investment Returns: So, Did You *Really* Keep Up with the Joneses?	11
2	Dollar-Cost Averaging: Financial Vitamin or Investment Placebo?	31
3	Home-Cooked Portfolio Insurance: Can You Invest Your Cake and Eat It Too?	49
4	Variable Annuities: An Investment to Die For?	65
5	Diversification: What's Wrong with One Basket?	87
6	Investing on Margin: The Good, the Bad, and the Ugly	107
7	Asset Allocation After Retirement: How to Avoid Outliving Your Money	117
8	Life Annuities: It's Not Now or Never	139
9	No Regrets: What Is a Risky Future?	165
	Notes	*181*
	Index	*189*

Acknowledgments

This book would have been impossible to produce without the inspiration and motivation of many friends and colleagues.

Each of the chapters that follow is the result of research projects that I have worked on, am working on, or hope to work on with various colleagues in and around the Schulich School of Business at York University in Toronto, Canada. With that in mind, I would like to thank my co-researchers, both past and present, for their insight and ideas. Specifically, they are Narat Charupat, Kwok Ho, Sharon Kim, Steven Posner, David Promislow, Eliezer Prisman, Chris Robinson, Tom Salisbury, and Hans Tuenter.

In addition, I would like to thank Scott Anderson, Lowell Aronoff, Joel Diena, David Fowler, Aron Gottesman, François Nault, Georges Monette, and Ron Uitz for commenting on the individual chapters as they were being created.

Special mention must go to Glenn Daily, who over the years has served as a virtual encyclopedia for detailed practitioner information about finance and insurance.

I would also like to thank the team at FMG in Toronto,

especially the boss, who many years ago hired an eager 13-year-old for a summer job in modern finance — he's been hooked ever since. I am also grateful to the folks at TIAA-CREF in New York City, who got me interested in actuarial problems and have supported my research over the years.

On the business side of things, I would like to thank my agent David Lavin at the DLA for introducing me to my wonderful co-author and urging me to undertake this project while arranging all the details — both big and small. This let me tend to what I love best, which is the research.

The editorial staff at Stoddart deserves a distinct mention, with special thanks to Marnie Kramarich for her marvelous assistance with the manuscript.

Finally, I cannot find the words to thank my beautiful and talented wife, Edna Ida, for her unconditional love, patience, and tolerance over the years. In addition to the millions of other things she does so successfully, she found the time to read, critique, and guide each and every chapter.

MOSHE A. MILEVSKY

God does not play dice
with the world.

— ALBERT EINSTEIN

INTRODUCTION

What Are the Odds?

A few months ago, I walked into my local bookstore and counted eight full bookshelves devoted to the subject of personal finance and investment counseling. The book topics covered the complete spectrum — how to pick good stocks, how to choose mutual funds that pick good stocks, how to select a financial planner who will help you choose a mutual fund that will pick good stocks. There were books on mortgages, minimizing taxes, maximizing estates, managing IRA and 401(k) plans, and winding down tax-sheltered plans. In total, I found more than 100 books offering financial planning advice.

So why, you are perfectly entitled to ask, am I writing another book on personal finance?

The answer is that I'm not. Certainly, it's not a personal

finance book of the ordinary kind. Let's get this straight right away. This book will not help you predict the next "big" thing or sidestep the next bear market. This book will not tell you how to find the next superstar mutual fund manager, nor will it identify which mutual fund will be the top performer in the next quarter. This book will not tell you the cheapest place to live, the real estate properties that are most likely to appreciate, or the tax shelter that is least likely to fall prey to the IRS.

I won't pretend to tell you any of that because, quite frankly, I can't. The simple truth is that none of us can accurately predict the future. The future, like the weather, is completely random.

Until about 10 years ago, you may recall, your local weather outlook consisted of a simple categorical prediction of whether it would be sunny, cloudy, rainy, or snowy. Statements such as "today it will rain," "tomorrow will be sunny," or "Thursday morning it will snow" were as sophisticated as the reports ever became. Of course, most weather forecasters got it wrong, and the art of weather prediction, which seemed to be based largely on *The Old Farmer's Almanac*, never garnered much respect.

Then, in the mid-1980s, things started to change. Hand in hand with the development of modern computer technology and the success of the scientific method, the art of weather prediction matured into the science of weather forecasting. Now, you can turn on the weather channel in the morning or log on to the Internet to learn about a given day's probability of precipitation (POP). Weather forecasters and their computers use what they know about the science of meteorology to convert today's temperature, humidity, and atmospheric pressure into tomorrow's probability of rain. You take the POP and make decisions accordingly.

Technically speaking, the probability of precipitation tells you the chances that it will rain more than 0.02 milliliters in a particular region. A 100% POP for today basically means that you can expect it to rain and you should definitely take your umbrella and raincoat to work. A 0% POP obviously means that the sky is completely clear and you can rest assured that it will not rain today. Any number above 0%, of course, represents a greater likelihood of rain. The higher the number, the greater the chance of precipitation.

As such, weather forecasters now have more flexibility. They don't have to make definitive predictions, which almost always end up being wrong. Instead, they can focus on the probability. Hence, if today's POP is 40% or higher, you would probably carry an umbrella. If the POP is lower than 40%, you'd probably leave the raingear at home. The decision about whether or not to take the umbrella takes into account the essential uncertainty of the weather and your attitude toward risk. The very conservative crowd might tote an umbrella whenever the POP is higher than 10%. Those who can handle a bit of rain-risk will have a higher POP threshold.

Why am I going on in this fashion about the weather? Because the underlying theme of this book involves precisely the same concepts of decision, uncertainty, and risk. You, the investor, often face a choice between two mutually exclusive courses of action — to take an umbrella (i.e., a financially conservative action) or not. And you must make the decision right now, knowing full well that in a day or a week or a month, you may regret not having made exactly the opposite decision.

Many financial decisions are like that. They consist of an either/or component, where each outcome is uncertain, hindsight is 20/20, and the regret is painful. Should I invest in safe certificates of deposit (CDs) at the local bank or should I invest in the stock market? Should I invest one lump sum, or smaller, equal amounts over time (a formula known as dollar-cost averaging)? Should I purchase a variable annuity or a basic mutual fund? Should I annuitize my nest egg at retirement or manage the assets myself? Obviously, you want to make these decisions armed with as much information as possible. The more you know, the better the odds that you won't experience financial loss and regret down the road.

This book is about helping you make informed decisions. More specifically, it's about using scientific methods to examine the odds involved in personal financial decisions. And it's about selecting a course of action that will maximize your long-term satisfaction. Of course, when the dice are finally rolled, you may still experience regret. Nothing is ever guaranteed. But at least you will have done the best you could do with the information you had.

Let me give you an example of how to examine the odds in the context of personal finance.

Imagine that you've just received a windfall inheritance from a distant relative. You decide to pay off some bills and, having done so, you discover that you still have $10,000 left over. You don't really need the money right now, so you decide to put it away for a rainy day.

You call up your financial adviser and ask: "What should I do with the $10,000? Should I put it all into a well-diversified index fund? Or should I play it safe and buy a certificate of deposit at my local bank?"

Of course, the prudent response on the part of your financial adviser or investment broker would be to suggest some form of diversification; after all, he or she might say, you don't want to put all your eggs in one basket. Depending on your risk tolerance, long-term goals, and financial position, you should probably split the money into various piles and certainly not restrict yourself to the all-or-nothing bank deposit or stock market choice.

But let's examine the all-or-nothing question in greater detail, focusing on the two extreme alternatives. If you "take the plunge" and invest the $10,000 in the stock market, what are the odds that you will regret this decision? What is the probability that the stock market is the wrong place to invest your money?

In a sense, you may have noticed, those questions are really pointless. They are pointless because no meaningful answer can be determined unless we specify an appropriate investment holding period. If you take the plunge, will you regret the decision tomorrow? Will you regret the decision in one year? Will you regret the decision in 10 years?

When do you need the money?

Figure: I.1 The Probability of Regret

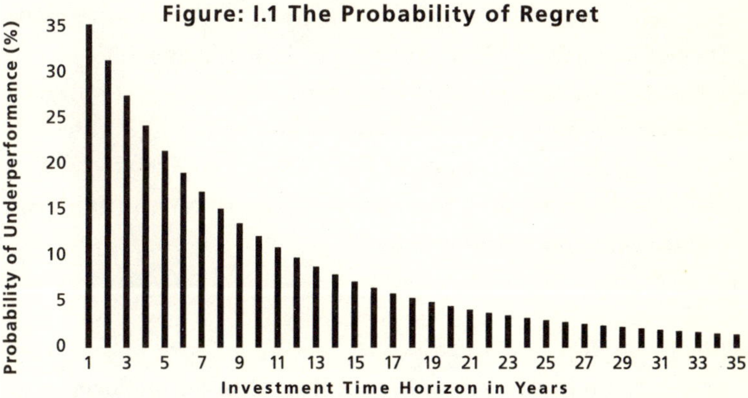

Figure I.1 illustrates what I call the time-adjusted "probability of financial regret." Over a one-year time horizon, it shows that there is a 35% chance that a diversified portfolio of U.S. equities will underperform the 5% rate of return from the safe bank deposit. Thus, if you're going to need the money in one year, there's a 35% chance that you will regret taking the stock market plunge. But what if you won't need the money for 10 years? In that case, the chart shows that a diversified portfolio of U.S. equities has just an 11% probability of shortfall. In other words, there's a better than four-in-five chance that, over the next decade, the U.S. stock market will experience a rate of return that is greater than the return currently available from a secure 5% bank deposit. As we will see in later chapters, the probability of actually losing money in the stock market — getting less than your original principal back after 10 years — is considerably lower than 11%; it's actually about 5%.

But we are not content with just the return of principal. Our regret benchmark is much higher. We want to beat the risk-free investment alternative, which is the bank deposit. We want to look back with hindsight and feel that we did the right thing.

Finally, what if your time horizon is 35 years away? In this case, the chart indicates a probability of financial regret of roughly 1%. As the time horizon increases, the probability of shortfall decreases rapidly; scientists like to say that it decays exponentially. It never actually hits zero — there are no guarantees in life — but it gets very close to zero. As we shall see later in the book, time and financial risk are intricately intertwined.

Table I.1

The Probability of Regret

Time Horizon in Years	Probability of Underperformance*
1	34.83%
2	29.06%
3	24.97%
4	21.77%
5	19.16%
10	10.87%
20	4.06%
25	2.56%
30	1.63%
35	1.05%

**Broad portfolio of U.S. equities with 5% benchmark*

Why is time so important? Let me give you an analogy. Let's say that a police officer stops you on the highway. He says you were clocked at 80 miles, and have broken the law. He starts to write you a ticket. Is the ticket justified? Well, that depends. If you were driving 80 miles per hour, you were going too fast and you deserve the speeding ticket. If, on the other hand, you were driving 80 miles per three hours, you were driving much too slowly, in which case you will probably get the ticket for holding up traffic! The point I'm trying to make is that, by itself, the 80 miles figure is meaningless. To give it genuine meaning, we must know the appropriate unit of time.

In a similar manner, financial risk has an embedded dimension of time. It is meaningless to talk about whether or not something is risky or safe without addressing the relevant time horizon and the financial alternatives. Indeed, over a one-year horizon, the stock market is clearly quite risky — relative to the secure alternative of putting the money in a CD. That's because the probability of shortfall, or regret from investing in stocks, is 35%.

On the other hand, if you adopt a 35-year horizon, the stock market is quite safe, relative to the CD alternative. That's because the probability of regret would then be about 1%. The flip side of this implies a strong probability of success, of having made the right choice. That probability is close to 99%.

In fact, I would argue that over a 35-year horizon, the bank deposit, or the money market fund, for that matter, is the risky asset class and the equity mutual fund is the safe asset class, especially when you look at it on an after-tax basis. But the main idea is that you should examine the odds that are attached to various courses of action.

You might be wondering, how, exactly, did I arrive at these probabilities? Well, I'm glad you asked. I borrowed a technique developed by scientists over the last few decades to deal with complicated questions in nuclear physics. It's called the method of Monte Carlo simulation, and these days, it's used in everything from traffic control to designing better soap. Let me explain how it works in more detail, since you will probably be seeing much more of this in the near future.

As part of the Mathematics of Individual Finance and Insurance Decisions (MiFiD) project at York University's Business School, some colleagues and I constructed a computer program that generates millions of different scenarios for the evolution of financial markets, interest rates, and inflation. It is, if you like, the ultimate imagination machine. Some scenarios show the stock market booming for the next 20 years; others indicate a 10-year bear market. The probabilities — or relative occurrences — for these "futures" are generated using historical statistical estimates.

Indeed, simulations of future market behavior have been employed quite successfully in corporate risk management, when a company wants to compute the probability of losing a specific amount of money over a particular time horizon. Government regulators also use the Monte Carlo method to estimate and measure the stability of the financial system.

As you might have guessed, the name Monte Carlo itself comes from the underlying roulette wheel in the computer that generates the different scenarios. It may sound a bit removed to let a computer determine what the future will look like, but with its exhaustive search ability, the program does survey all possible contingencies, every possible financial scenario of what could happen in the future.

True, no computer could have predicted the collapse of the Asian economies or the debt default of the Russian government. The point is not to identify or predict specific events; rather, it is to compute all possibilities for the evolution of the financial markets. The real trick is to get the computer to generate reasonable and accurate scenarios for the future, without falling prey to the fallacy that history will repeat itself.

Once the millions of scenarios have been generated, we start counting. This is how we can calculate the odds.

That's exactly what we'll do in the following pages. Using the Monte Carlo simulation, I want to help you examine the odds for choices you face in your day-to-day financial life. By conducting these simulations I can tell you the probability that you will regret a particular decision or course of action.

Once you know the odds, you can make a more informed decision, which is why this book is titled *The Probability of Fortune: Financial Strategies with the Best Odds*. Among other topics, the book will investigate and focus on the following subjects:

CHAPTER 1
What are the odds that your wonderful mutual fund manager was just lucky?

CHAPTER 2
Should you invest according to dollar-cost averaging or in one lump sum?

CHAPTER 3
Can you create investment protection yourself, by "cooking" portfolio insurance at home?

CHAPTER 4
Variable annuities offer a unique form of investment insurance. What is the value of this protection and how much should you be willing to pay for it?

CHAPTER 5
How many stocks should you or your mutual fund hold in order to be considered diversified? Why is diversification so important?

CHAPTER 6
Should you borrow money and use leverage to invest in the stock market?

CHAPTER 7
At retirement, should you shift your investments into safe, income-producing assets or should you maintain some exposure to the stock market?

CHAPTER 8
Should you convert your 401(k), IRA, and other retirement savings plans into a life annuity or manage your own systematic withdrawal plan?

CHAPTER 9
What is financial risk?

The common factors in all of these questions are the elements of decision, risk probability, and uncertainty. As you can imagine, you can mount a well-argued case for each side of the coin, but you can't act until you know the odds.

This book will help you determine the odds, and let you decide if you need to take the umbrella.

I hope you enjoy — and profit.

CHAPTER

1

Your Investment Returns:

So, Did You *Really* Keep Up with the Joneses?

Congratulations! You just received your quarterly mutual fund statement in the mail and, miracle of miracles, you've actually made a few dollars. In fact, since the last time you checked, your investment has earned quite a handsome return. If this keeps up, you say to yourself, you might be able to retire at age 55 and sail around the world in that yacht you've always wanted.

You're just about to compliment yourself on a wonderful choice of mutual fund — and perhaps even send the fund manager a bouquet of fresh chrysanthemums — when you ponder an innocent question: How well did the competition do? After all, who among us doesn't find it far more enjoyable to make money when you know that everyone else hasn't made as much? So you check the mutual fund rankings from your favorite financial newspaper and find that the median fund in that category earned a full three percentage points less than your fund over the last 12 months. Indeed, over the last quarter, your fund beat the median fund by 1.5% (or 150 basis points). Now you are definitely ready to celebrate. True, a few funds did perform somewhat better than yours, including one that had been recommended to you; you're slightly annoyed to see that it's the top-ranked fund in that category. But you're not greedy. You beat the average. You picked a good, solid fund, run by a skillful manager, and you did well.

Or did you?

The questions you might be tempted to ask are: What are the odds that your fund's fine performance was simply a fluke? What are the odds that you were simply lucky? How can you tell — in a scientific fashion — if your fund manager actually turned in a stellar performance or if he or she (and you) were simply the beneficiaries of enormous good fortune?

Those are the questions I will try to answer here. Specifically, I will examine the issues that you should consider when trying to distinguish true fund-management skill from random, good luck.

Demonstrating genuine and consistent skill in fund management is, I submit, a very difficult art. Let me explain why I think so. The challenge most fund managers face in outperforming the passive stock indexes — and the reason for my skepticism about claims of any future ability to do so — is exemplified by the following statistics. According to Morningstar Inc., a total of 5,296 mutual funds (as of December 31, 1999) were classified with a mandate to invest in diversified U.S. equities. Of those 5,296 funds, however, only 396 have been in existence long enough to have a 15-year track record. The performance record of these 396 mutual fund veterans has varied widely. The best of them earned a compound annual return of 26.69% over the 15 years. An investment with this top-performing superstar would have effectively multiplied your money by a factor of 35. The worst performance record of the 15-year veterans was a compound annual return of –7.02%. I don't even want to get into what taxes, transaction costs, and front- or back-end loads would have done to that fund.

So the range for these 396 players was –7.02% to 26.69% during the 15-year period. Moreover, the median fund — half fell above and half fell below — in this category earned approximately 15.34%. But here is the other side of the story: over exactly the same period, the passive (no-brainer) S&P 500 index earned 18.92%, and the broader Wilshire 5000 index earned 18.12%. This is almost 3% more than the median return for the 396 funds. Furthermore, if you examine the individual performances of these 396 funds, you will see that only 81 were able to beat the Wilshire 5000 and only 64 were able to beat the S&P 500. In other words, between 80% and 85% of mutual funds with 15-year track records underperformed the index. Clearly, then, the historical odds of beating the index are not great.

Now, granted, some of you may question the comparison of these funds to the broad index. Indeed, some of these funds were investing in only a small segment of the market. But you could perform a similar analysis with any index that you deemed appropriate. The fact is that no matter what index you use — S&P, Dow, or Russell — the numbers are quite similar. Much fewer than half of the players beat the (appropriate) index averages. Part of this result can be explained by the transaction costs involved with mutual funds, costs that a passive index does not incur. But the margin of underperformance is still too large.

I suspect that when a fund has a consistently appalling or embarrassing performance record, its sponsors try to kill it — by either merging it with a more successful fund, changing its mandate, or simply closing it down. What this means to you as an investor is that the 396 funds with 15-year track records are a small portion of the much larger universe of mutual funds that once hoped to create their own impressive 15-year track records — and gave up trying. In other words, the 396 funds are merely the survivors of the grueling mutual fund wars. And what you're looking at, therefore, is a biased group of funds.

It's like saying that the average Boston marathon runner completed the race in two hours and 47 minutes. Sure, those who completed the course did it in two hours and 47 minutes, on average. But what about all those runners who dropped out? Clearly, the survivors have better records than the dropouts or losers.

What this means for mutual funds is that the true 15-year performance record of all those funds that initially tried to create a strong record (finish the marathon) is much worse than that of the survivors. The true median for this larger group is certainly lower than 15.34%.

Looking ahead, I interpret this data to mean that your odds of finding a fund that will outperform benchmark averages over the next 15 years are even lower than recorded history would suggest.

Now, please don't get the wrong impression. I am most certainly not against buying or investing in mutual funds. I invest in them myself because, among other numerous benefits, they reduce transaction costs and expenses by pooling purchases. And for those investors who don't have the time to search for good stocks, mutual funds do the job for them.

However, and here is my pitch, I don't necessarily invest in mutual funds with the intention or hope of beating the competition. I also put a fund's performance record through a battery of tests — some of which you will read about below — before I am willing to convince myself that the manager was not just lucky.

Now, you may wonder at this point, does it really matter? After all, the past is history. The fact is, you did well. The fund's performance was better than average. Who cares why?

Well, this is where I respectfully disagree. If the past can be attributed to mere chance, then there is really nothing intrinsically adroit or wise or skillful about your fund manager. More importantly, there is no guarantee that this great performance will be repeated. Of course, even if your manager has been skillful, there is certainly no guarantee that this skill will continue. But if your manager is diagnosed as just lucky, then your chance of repeating success — of beating the competition again — is basically 50/50.

With this in mind, I would argue that the "Monday morning quarterback" diagnosis is extremely important when it comes to making decisions about future investments. If your manager is found to have above-average stock-picking skills, you're likely to feel more comfortable entrusting him or her with even more of your hard-earned money. Certainly, you won't feel as bad paying 0.50% (or more) of your money each year for the manager's work.

If, on the other hand, it's simply luck, you will probably think twice.

Before we dive into the technical details, a few general statements are in order. Clearly — and you certainly don't need me to tell you this — the longer and the more consistently your fund performs above the average, the more justified you are in considering your fund manager a skillful stock picker. In other words, one good year does not imply any remarkable skill, especially if all the other years were lousy.

Warren Buffett and Peter Lynch, among other famous investors, have demonstrated astonishing stock-picking skills, and have been phenomenally consistent over long periods of time. There is no question that their performance must be attributed to investment acumen; it cannot be dismissed as mere lady luck. True, Mr. Buffett's Berkshire Hathaway investment return during 1999 left much to be desired. But one or two bad years should not be taken as evidence of lousy investment acumen, just as one or two years of phenomenal gains cannot be taken as evidence of superior skills. In fact, that is exactly what we are trying to determine.

The question at hand is: How long — and how far above average — must a fund manager's successful record be before we can declare him or her as having turned in a performance that transcends the realm of chance?

At this point I need to declare a bias. Given the enormous competition that exists in the marketplace, and given the sheer number of individual analysts and institutions that are searching for undervalued stocks, I am somewhat skeptical about anyone's ability to consistently beat the market, to consistently do better than average. Somewhere between 60% and 70% of all mutual funds — depending on the period reviewed — fail to beat the stock market averages in the long run. In plain English, consistently successful stock picking is a very tough job, and my hat goes off to those who truly manage to outperform.

Let me clarify what I mean. There are (usually) 500 stocks in the S&P 500 index. Think of it for the moment — please forgive the gambling analogy — as the equivalent of 500 horses at the local racetrack. From this list of 500, mutual fund managers pick between 30 and 50 of their favorite and most promising stocks. But if these managers are truly skillful stock-pickers, why do most of them — as anyone can see from quarterly mutual fund rankings — deliver fund performances that are worse than the market-value average performance of those same 500 stocks?

Even when you account for transaction costs, fees, and a commission, the typical fund manager still underperforms the stock market averages. This is not like major league baseball where any athlete can hit, run, and throw better than you and I could ever hope to. It appears that we have many professional fund managers, analysts, stockbrokers, and traders who simply can't — or don't — do better than your ordinary investor who picks a collection of random stocks from the New York Stock Exchange and other national and international markets. In no other professional association can you find so many members who fail to display the basic skills on which the association is founded.

Why?

The reason for this is simple: The members of this association — principally, stock analysts — are competing fiercely against each other to locate hidden and undervalued investments.

The one who succeeds must succeed at the expense of all the others, who failed to locate the same undervalued investment. The one who gets there first must win at the expense of all the others, who were too slow out of the gate.

Now, as the number of active stock analysts increases, and the number of mutual funds expands, the odds of this happening — consistently, I might add — will continue to decline. This fact goes a long way toward explaining the growth of such passively managed investment products as index funds, WEBS, Spiders, and Country Baskets, which are available on the New York and American Stock Exchanges and have a simple mandate to match or replicate the market average.

With the odds of successful outperformance continuing to decline, many investors feel that if you can't beat 'em, join 'em.

Ironically, in the very long term, if too many investors become disillusioned, shift their wealth, and adopt passive investment strategies that simply mimic the broader indices, there will be fewer analysts actively searching for value and the possibility of outperformance — or of finding neglected values — will once again increase.

Therefore, if I have a bias — and I do admit one — it is that I don't believe in the widespread existence of such enduring stock-picking skills. To be convinced of true talent in this field, I require compelling evidence. It is not very different from the scientist who begins with an underlying hypothesis — or assumption — about the world at large. To invalidate the hypothesis, the scientist must uncover strong evidence that is inconsistent with the hypothesis and that cannot be attributed to chance alone.

My personal bias is known — and referred to by economists — as the Efficient Market Hypothesis. The EMH, as it is sometimes known, postulates that markets are efficient in the sense that it is very difficult or even impossible to consistently earn above-average investment returns without taking on excessive levels of risk. We will get to the risk issue in a moment.

Consider the following analogy. Your youngest daughter, your precious eight-year-old, is having her birthday party next week. In addition to all the usual elements, like cake, balloons, etc., you decide to hire the latest fad in children's entertainment — the professional CoinTosser. Although his fee is a little steep, the CoinTosser promises to make your party a memorable one by repeatedly tossing a coin in the air and consistently getting heads. No doubt, you think, he'll have the kids and adults oohing and aahing.

But there's a minor problem with hiring the CoinTosser. Although the local authorities tightly regulate the industry — CoinTossers must attend some classes and pass exams — there are, unfortunately, quite a few charlatans masquerading as professionals. These impostors claim to be able to toss many heads but, when push comes to shove, they disappoint the audience. Of course, they always manage to toss a few heads, but with far too many tails in between. But all of the CoinTossers, you have observed, are great marketers. Their advertisements are glitzy. They spend a small fortune on brochures, print ads, and television campaigns, and their fees continue to increase each year. They are all members of the Certified Flippers Association. Very few of them, however, seem to possess real, unchallengeable skills.

Being a perfectionist, you decide to interview a few of them before hiring one for your party. More specifically, you ask them to provide their historical track record of coin tosses at other parties so that you can determine whether they are truly adroit CoinTossers or just lucky.

In fact, to make the interview process more scientific, you ask your next-door neighbor, Tom the Mathematician, to provide you with the chances of coming up with a specific number of heads when a coin is tossed 10 times. This

Table 1.1

What are the odds of turning up different numbers of heads when tossing a coin 10 times?*

Number of Heads Tossed	Probability
0	0.00098
1	0.00977
2	0.04394
3	0.11719
4	0.20508
5	0.24608
6	0.20508
7	0.11719
8	0.04394
9	0.00977
10	0.00098

**The numbers should add up to exactly one, because all 11 possibilities are enumerated.*

way, you can determine whether or not the CoinTosser possesses genuine skill.

Tom shows you Table 1.1, and then explains how to read and interpret the numbers. For example, the probability of never getting heads when you toss 10 coins — in other words, tails every time — is 0.00098. That's slightly less than a one-in-a-thousand chance of throwing tails 10 times in a row.

Similarly, the probability of flipping eight heads — not necessarily in a row — when you toss a coin 10 times is 0.04394. This, Tom explains, is slightly more than a 4% chance. Clearly, the most likely outcome is five heads, which has a 0.24608 probability, or roughly a 25% chance of occurring. Notice the symmetry: the odds of flipping eight heads are the same as the chance of flipping two heads (i.e., eight tails). They are both 0.04394, about 4%.

You are now ready to interview the CoinTossers. Some are older, and have performed at many parties over the years; others look like they just graduated from college. (The common denominator seems to be that they all wear very expensive clothes.) For consistency and comparison, you ask them to provide the results achieved at their last party.

Candidate Number One comes in with a track record of seven heads — out of 10 tosses — from his last engagement. You look again at Tom's table and see that the likelihood of getting seven heads, out of 10, is 0.11719, which is roughly a 12% chance. According to Tom, this means there's a 12% probability that this CoinTosser's track record is attributable to chance. Stated differently, if a charlatan CoinTosser with absolutely no tossing skills performed this party trick at 100 different parties — tossing 10 coins at each party — then one would expect him to toss seven heads at 12 parties.

The challenge — once again — is to distinguish between

authentic skill and mere chance. Your underlying hypothesis is that they are all charlatans — or are simply misguided about their own abilities. To convince yourself otherwise, you require strong evidence. Is seven heads strong evidence? I would say no. Twelve percent is simply too high a number.

So what is the threshold? At what probability are we willing to reject our hypothesis and accept the fact that a particular CoinTosser must be quite skilled?

Over the years, statisticians have developed a cut-off point for distinguishing randomness from causality. The number is usually in the 5% region. More stringent cases require a number closer to 1%, and sometimes even 0.5%.

For example, when doctors test a new medical procedure or drug, it is natural for some patients to get better, for others to deteriorate, and for others still to stay the same. Those patients who improve may do so for reasons that have nothing to do with the new medication; in other words, it may just be chance. And those who decline may decline even though the treatment is beneficial. So how does the scientist determine whether to reject the hypothesis that it's all random?

For example, let's say the doctors administered the new treatment to 100 patients. Of these, 60 got better, 20 stayed the same, and 20 declined. How do we know if the medicine was really effective — and that those who improved did not do so simply by chance? To answer the question, doctors use a table much like Table 1.1, except that their data will indicate the chance that a certain number of patients got better — or worse — due to purely natural or random reasons. Clearly, the greater the number of patients that improved, the lower the likelihood is of this happening by chance alone.

So the answer, once again, depends on the odds. In the case of a medical procedure, if there is less than a 1%

chance of these improvements occurring for natural reasons, the scientist rejects the randomness hypothesis and attributes the outcome to causality, i.e., he concludes that his patients improved as a result of the new treatment. If, on the other hand, the odds of this outcome are greater than 1%, the hypothesis is not rejected. Even though many patients may be better, the scientist cannot be assured that their turn-around was not simply a matter of pure chance, or that it was outside the realm of natural randomness.

But you can clearly see the bias. The original hypothesis must be overturned in order to accept the legitimacy of the medical procedure. You can't really prove or disprove a natural assertion of this sort. The best you can do is find evidence that is consistent or inconsistent with your hypothesis.

In the birthday party analogy, only a very impressive track record can discredit the charlatan hypothesis. Only then will you accept the fact that your candidates are true professionals and have authentic coin-tossing skills.

For example, if Candidate Number Two shows a latest-party track record of nine heads — according to Table 1.1, this has less than a 1% chance of occurring randomly — you would almost certainly reject the hypothesis that this person is a charlatan. With the first candidate, you could not have the same degree of confidence. Candidate Number One, you'll recall, had a track record of seven heads (a 12% chance) — a number that would not allow you to reject the initial hypothesis that he has no intrinsic skill. Of course, he may in fact be very skillful, and may simply have had a bad day at the last party. But the track record is not enough to change your basic convictions.

Although it may be somewhat harsh to compare mutual fund managers to CoinTossers, the methodology for determining skill is essentially the same.

Remember, many different mutual fund managers and

companies are competing for your investment dollars. Some have been in the business for many years. Others are brand new to the game. All implicitly promise — and certainly hope — to do better than their competitors and to beat the market averages. Their historical track records are crucial to their pitch. What should you be looking at? What are the odds that they were just lucky?

The first thing you must do is compare them with the appropriate competition, benchmark, and stock index. If they have a mandate to invest in natural resource companies, you (and they) should not be comparing their performance with the financial services sector. Likewise, if they invest only in European stocks, you should not compare their performance with the U.S., Latin America, or the Far East.

In many cases, however, the benchmarking comparison is easier said than done. What about balanced equity and bond funds? What about small-cap funds? What about social investing funds? What about funds with a broad investment mandate? What benchmarks do you use to compare, monitor, and confirm their investment skills? Needless to say, these questions are not easily answered. Indeed, a cottage industry of performance consultants has been created to fill this niche. Trustees of public and private pension funds are required to monitor the relative — not just absolute — performance of their funds. I can, however, tell you that both fund regulators and consumer advocates are pressuring fund companies and managers to do a better job — in their shareholder reports and initial prospectuses — of telling investors how they performed relative to the passive and active competition.

Using our coin-tossing lingo, if a mutual fund performed better than the index average, I will call that "heads"; if it did worse than the average, I will call that "tails."

Let's say that a fund has been in existence for 10 years

— i.e., it has a 10-year track record — and that it performed better than the appropriate benchmark for seven of those 10 years. During the other three years, by implication, it did worse than the benchmark average. Ignoring for the moment the amount or relative magnitude of the over- and underperformance, let's focus on the probability that this performance is consistent with the starting hypothesis of zero stock-picking skill. What are the odds that a fund manager with no skill — but a lot of luck — will be able to outperform the stock market averages for seven out of 10 years?

Once again, Table 1.1 gives us the answer — 12%. Is this number too high or too low? Remember, the lower the number, the more impressive the performance, and the less likely I am to attribute it to chance alone. Therefore, as I argued in the coin-tossing case, 12% is not low enough to make me reject my original hypothesis that the performance can be attributed to mere luck.

Now, had the performance been above the average in nine out of 10 years, Table 1.1 would give us a number around 1%, which is very impressive. In other words, if the manager has absolutely no stock-picking skills, the chances of his being above average nine out of 10 years are less than 1%. Such a performance would cause me to reject my randomness hypothesis and declare the manager as having bona fide skill.

Of course, there is nothing magical about 10 years. The same approach can be taken with any historical performance record. If a fund has been in existence for 15 years, you can compute the chances of getting 10 above-average years (it's about 9%). Therefore, a fund manager with absolutely no skill can be expected to produce a 10-for-15 track record 9% of the time. Once again, this performance (10-for-15) is not enough in my judgment to reject the randomness hypothesis.

Now, you might ask, why am I so tough to please? After all, a batting average of 10-for-15 isn't exactly bad. In major league baseball, it would be considered a real accomplishment. Why isn't 10-for-15 impressive when it comes to stock picking? Why is my investment bar set so high? Well, remember, you and I would probably bat 0-for-15 against any major league pitcher. But we could probably score a decent 7-for-15 against the stock market averages. That's because the chances are that by simply picking stocks haphazardly, half the time we would do better than the stock market averages, half the time we would do worse. This is why a mutual fund investment average of 10-for-15, though certainly respectable, isn't really that impressive. It definitely isn't enough to overturn my good-luck hypothesis. We must remember the litmus test — how far is this outcome from the no-skill case?

Ten-for-fifteen looks okay until you begin to examine the track record of investment demigods. For example, it's estimated that the legendary Warren Buffett has a 22-for-25 record. This means that he outperformed market averages in 22 of 25 years of investing.

What are the odds of this occurring through mere chance? The answer: about one in 50,000. That, to me, is strong evidence consistent with the premise that he's a talented investor. Of course, true skeptics would argue that every group of 50,000 investors should produce one Warren Buffett on average — simply as a result of chance. But there is another factor to consider; while Mr. Buffett's ability to repeatedly beat the index is impressive, the *amount by which* he has done so each year is even more amazing.

This brings me to the many caveats and disclaimers in my simple perspective.

First and foremost, I have completely ignored the amount by which these track records beat or failed to beat the average, i.e., the magnitude of over- and underperformance. There's no denying that the performance of a Warren Buffett or a Peter Lynch is more impressive than their success rate — narrowly defined — would indicate. That's because the amount by which they have outperformed the averages is also inconsistent with a randomness hypothesis.

Indeed, all fund managers who "bat" 7-for-10 are not alike. Some manage to outperform the averages by a large margin. Others barely exceed the benchmark by a percentage point or two. Obviously, the higher the margin, the more likely I am to declare them skillful.

In practice, therefore, we need a table that is slightly more complicated than Table 1.1. We need a probability table that takes into account the magnitude of the over- and underperformance.

More importantly, a money market fund manager who outperforms the category average by a full percentage point is much more impressive than an international equity fund manager who outperforms the average by 1%. The higher volatility in the latter category implies a wide variation in performance with some funds doing much better and some much worse than average. On the other hand, the very low volatility in returns on money market funds, which tend to yield a clustering of performance numbers, makes a 1% margin quite remarkable. Therefore, when examining the magnitude of outperformance, it's crucial to consider — or adjust for — the level of volatility or fluctuations in that particular category. Industry analysts refer to this — and you may have heard the term — as adjusting performance for risk.

Although the underlying mathematics can be daunting, Table 1.2 provides a rough sense of how the outperformance chances stack up. Specifically, and without getting into too much detail, I classify three distinct categories of mutual fund volatility or fluctuation factors: low, medium, and high. You might think of low volatility as a money market or short-term bond fund. Medium volatility might be a balanced fund, comprising both equity and bonds in roughly the same proportions. High volatility corresponds to a pure equity fund, invested both in the U.S. and internationally. Remember that the lower the volatility, the more impressive is a fixed outperformance margin.

Table 1.2

What are the chances of exceeding benchmark averages at different volatility levels?

	Low	Med	High
Outperformance Margin			
50 bp*	23.97%	36.18%	42.98%
100 bp	7.86%	23.97%	36.18%
200 bp	0.23%	7.86%	23.97%
250 bp	0.02%	3.85%	18.84%
500 bp	0.00%	0.02%	3.85%
600 bp	0.00%	0.00%	1.69%

**"bp" stands for basis points. One basis point is equal to 1/100 of a percentage point. Statistically speaking, in order of magnitude, low volatility is 5%, medium volatility is 10%, and high volatility is 20%. A probability of 0.00% does not mean that it is impossible, but rather that the number's first three digits are zero.*

For example, a low-volatility money market mutual fund that manages to earn a one-year return of 6% when the index average was 5.5% has exceeded the benchmark by a margin of 50 basis points. The probability of this occurring — assuming that the manager has no particular skill — is roughly 24%. Not very impressive. Furthermore, the probability of another "unskillful" manager in the same category earning 6.5% (100 basis points above the average) is a much lower 8%. This number sounds more promising. The higher the margin of outperformance, the lower the probability.

In fact, at some point, the margin gets so high — roughly

at 150 basis points for the low-volatility fund — that we must reject the hypothesis of randomness and conclude that the manager truly is skillful. This is akin to the CoinTosser flipping nine heads out of 10 — or a fund manager outperforming the index nine years out of 10; in both instances, due to the low probability, we reject the hypothesis of randomness and attribute the performance to skill. In one example, we were looking at investment returns over many years, strictly in terms of success and failure. In this case, we are looking at the investment return from any particular year.

Interestingly, the same 100-basis-point margin of outperformance doesn't appear impressive at all when the fund happens to be in the medium- or high-volatility category. Remember, the lower the probability number, the more impressive the result. In fact, in the medium and high categories, you need a much greater outperformance number before the findings can be dismissed as being attributable to pure chance. In the medium-volatility category, for example, a 250-basis-point margin (and in the high-volatility category, a 500-basis-point margin) is the point at which I would get excited. The reason is simple. High volatility leads to lower levels of clustering in investment returns. As such, there is a greater likelihood of exceeding — and, analogously, falling short of — the benchmarks by higher amounts.

Remember, though, that we are looking at an investment return for a single year. A medium-volatility fund manager who can (a) exceed the benchmark for seven years out of 10, but at the same time (b) outperform the benchmark by 200 basis points in any one year, is performing in a way that is extremely unlikely and highly improbable with no investment skill. Although separately both events (a) and (b) could be attributed to randomness, the combination of the two events definitely could not.

Bear in mind that I do not want to create a false sense of precision with these numbers. Indeed, simple volatility may not be the only factor to examine when adjusting for risk; and the margin of outperformance is not the only concern. How tax-effective is the fund? How liquid are the investments? How high are the expense ratios? As a consultant who has worked in this industry, I can assure you that benchmarking and measuring outperformance is a complicated — and many times contentious — process. But the underlying intuition is as follows: True skill is very hard to measure, and the odds should be examined with caution.

CONCLUSION

There are three levels of investment performance to be expected from mutual fund managers. First and foremost — by accepting fluctuating stock market risk — you can unquestionably demand to surpass the long-term rate of return from a risk-free investment in bank certificates of deposit, money market funds, or U.S. Savings Bonds.

Second, by entrusting your money to a particular mutual fund company or money manager, it is not unreasonable to request that they toss more heads than tails — in other words, repeatedly do better than the stock market averages. Otherwise, why bother with active management? You could simply buy a passive index investment, or do it yourself by picking your own stocks.

Third, and finally, in exchange for those high management expenses, front- and back-end loads, and other service charges, you should insist that your fund manager outperform the appropriate index averages by a statistically significant margin. In short, any fund manager should display a track record that is undeniably attributable to skill.

With that in mind, you and your financial planner should

always be cognizant of the main question: What are the odds that this performance can be attributed to simple chance alone? Remember, the lower the number, the more valuable the service provided by the manager.

CHAPTER

2

Dollar-Cost Averaging:

Financial Vitamin or Investment Placebo?

Eat well, exercise regularly, and invest according to the principles of dollar-cost averaging. Such are the maxims of advice doled out repeatedly in our national media. I really can't quibble with the first two; the medical evidence is overwhelming. But I do have very serious concerns about the third strategy.

It never ceases to amaze me how popular and widespread the practice of dollar-cost averaging has become. According to conventional wisdom, it's the key to a long and prosperous life — the investment equivalent of a healthy diet and regular exercise. Indeed, this mantra has now been repeated so many times that it has become virtually axiomatic.

But is dollar-cost averaging really everything it's cracked

up to be? My goal in this chapter is to answer exactly that question — to examine the odds of successful dollar-cost averaging and to discuss the narrow conditions under which it makes sense and the many conditions under which it does not.

But let me state my bias clearly up front: My personal view, which I will try to support with solid facts, is that many alternative investment strategies give you far better odds than dollar-cost averaging.

For the record, dollar-cost averaging — also known simply as DCA — is a systematic investment strategy in which a fixed dollar amount is invested on a regular basis in a particular stock, mutual fund, or other asset class. For example, many American households, at the encouragement of their financial advisers, have implemented automatic monthly withdrawals from their bank accounts ($250, for example) that go directly into their favorite mutual fund(s).

Now, according to advocates of DCA, this method of forced savings has the benefit of buying more units when prices are lower and fewer units when prices are higher. The same $250 will buy 2.5 units of fund XYZ when it is selling at $100 per share, but only two units of fund XYZ when it is selling at $125 per share. So the cheaper the price, the more units you can buy; conversely, the more inflated or expensive the price, the fewer units you'll be able to acquire. This amounts to the first part of a "buy low, sell high" strategy.

To make dollar-cost averaging look even more impressive, one can demonstrate that after one year of implementing this strategy on a monthly basis, the average cost of the units you've acquired will actually be lower than the average monthly price of the units during the year. Using this approach, you have consistently bought into the fund at a lower-than-average historical price.

For example, after a year of investing $250 a month, you have a total outflow of $3,000. That's all you know for certain. The actual value of your portfolio at year-end may be higher or lower than $3,000, depending on how the units performed and what they are then worth. But one thing is mathematically guaranteed to be true: the average price you paid for those units — or the value of your portfolio at year-end divided by the number of units you are holding — will always be lower than the average month-end price of those same units. So, if you paid an average of $100 for the units, you can be sure that the average monthly price was higher than $100 over the year. If you paid an average of $150 per unit, you can be sure that the average monthly price was higher than $150. This is a mathematical certainty, because you always buy more units when prices are lower and fewer when prices are higher.

Similarly, if you cut down your caviar consumption when it's expensive and eat more when it's cheap, you will always end up paying less for your caviar compared to the average price. This is why the strategy is called dollar-cost averaging. Your investment is averaged into the market over the course of the year at a fixed cost each month.

So what, then, you might ask, is wrong with dollar-cost averaging? If you did this for a few years, effectively buying at below-average prices, your investment portfolio would be in very good shape. Wouldn't it?

Well, the answer depends on what you're measuring the strategy against. Compared with not saving or not investing at all, dollar-cost averaging is a wonderful idea. I'm solidly in favor of people taking care of their own needs and saving for long-term goals by putting money away on a regular basis. It's a sensible *modus operandi*. But it makes no sense to blindly recommend a specific financial strategy without looking at appropriate alternatives. Indeed, this philosophy applies not only to dollar-cost averaging, but to *any* investment tactic. The question then is this: with what can we compare DCA?

Well, I would like to compare dollar-cost averaging with a natural and symmetric alternative called lump-sum investing — or LSI for short.

For the sake of argument, let's suppose that you have $3,000 in cash, which you would like to invest in equity mutual fund XYZ. However, let's also assume that North American capital markets are at historically high valuation levels. Accordingly, you are debating whether to (a) invest the entire $3,000 right now in a lump sum, or (b) dollar-cost average the money into the market over the next year. Practically speaking, the DCA strategy would be implemented by placing the $3,000 in a money market fund — or even a simple interest-bearing checking account — and then transferring $250 each month (plus any accumulated interest), and acquiring as many units as you could afford of equity fund XYZ.

By the end of the year — under both strategies — the $3,000, plus or minus gains and losses, will be completely invested in equity fund XYZ. The main issue at hand can be stated as a simple question: Which of these two strategies is better? Is it true, as so many experts claim, that dollar-cost averaging is preferable and wiser?

Before we answer this question, let's make sure we understand exactly how dollar-cost averaging and lump-sum investing would look in practice.

Let's start with your $3,000 investment. The price of one unit of XYZ mutual fund is initially $100. The LSI investment strategy is pretty straightforward. Your $3,000 buys 30 units ($3,000 = 30 x $100) and you intend to hold them for the long term. At the end of the year, if the price of the unit is $125, you've made a profit of $750 (30 units x $25) on your initial investment of $3,000. That's a 25% return in one year — very respectable indeed — and corresponds to the 25% increase in the XYZ unit price. You participate fully in the percentage increase. Similarly, under LSI, if the price of the unit falls to $75, you lose $750 (30 x $25), and are left with a portfolio valued at $2,250 at the end of the year. Once again, you participate fully in the percentage decrease. One can therefore say that the volatility of your invested capital is equivalent to the volatility of the units.

However, with dollar-cost averaging, things become a bit more complicated. Now, the $3,000 is split into 12 segments. Each segment is invested — or used to acquire units — on a monthly basis. At inception (for argument's sake, January 1), the first segment of $250 buys 2.5 units at $100, which is the initial price. The remaining 11 segments are set aside (preferably in an interest-bearing account) to be used in the subsequent 11 months. On February 1, the second segment of $250, plus one month's accumulated interest on that amount, will be used to acquire additional units of XYZ.

Now, here's where the fun begins. If, on February 1, the value of XYZ units has fallen to $95, the $250 plus interest (say, $251.25, at half a percent per month) will buy 2.6447 units of the XYZ fund. This is more than the 2.5 units purchased in January, because the unit value has fallen. And the more XYZ has fallen, the greater the number of units you can acquire.

On the other hand, if the price of XYZ units rises to $105 by February 1, the same $251.25 will buy only 2.3928 units. This is obviously less than 2.5, because the value of XYZ has increased. So the more XYZ has increased, the fewer units you can acquire with the fixed $251.25.

Indeed, when the unit price increases by 5% to $105, the dollar-cost averaging investor — with only January's capital in the market — gains a meager 2.5 units x $5 = $12.50 on $3,000, not counting bank interest. The lump-sum investor, on the other hand, has gained a full 30 units x $5 = $150, which corresponds to the 5% increase in the fund's value.

The same principle, of course, applies on the downside. If the unit price decreases by 5%, to $95, the dollar-cost averaging investor loses only $12.50 on the original $3,000 investment (2.5 units x $5). The DCA investor's $3,000 has become $2,987.50, a reduction of a mere 0.4% (ignoring any interest from the bank account where the funds are waiting to be averaged in). The lump-sum investor, however, has lost $150 (30 units x $5), which is 5% of the $3,000 and precisely mirrors the 5% loss in unit value.

This phenomenon is widely referred to as the volatility reduction of dollar-cost averaging. DCA acts as a shock absorber on both the upside and the downside. As you saw in the example, you don't lose as much from DCA if the price falls, but you don't gain as much if it rises.

The process of buying piece by piece continues each and every month until all the remaining segments — plus any accumulated interest — are fully invested in units of XYZ. This slow yet methodical approach means that you gradually build up an exposure to the units of XYZ. In the meantime, your investment's sensitivity to changes in unit value is much less than one-for-one, until your capital is completely invested in the units. Indeed, the total value of your equity will not fluctuate as much as the underlying unit values. This, once again, is the reduction in volatility. Finally, when the 12 months are over, the shock absorbers are entirely removed and you are in the same boat as the lump-sum investor. Except, chances are, the lump-sum investor is sitting in the more comfortable bow and you are in the lagging stern.

Why?

Think about the big picture for a moment. There are three distinct possibilities that could ensue by the end of the year. In the first scenario, the unit price stays relatively flat over this period. In Figure 2.1, this is displayed with the price-path leading to the letter B. As you can see, give or

Figure 2.1 Price-Path of Stock

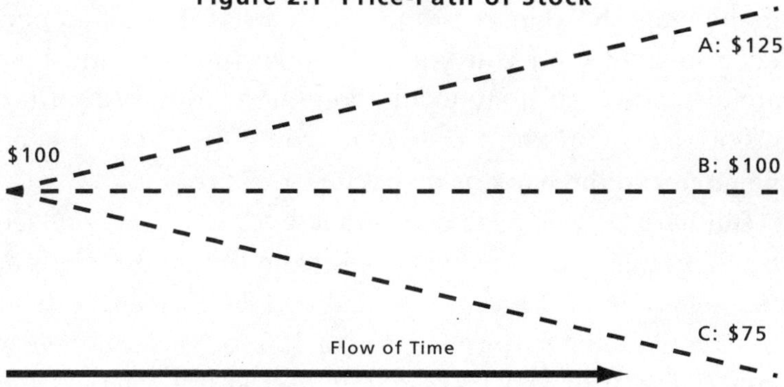

take a few dollars added or subtracted during its journey, the investment ends up at the same place it started — namely, at $100 per unit.

In the case outlined above, both DCA and LSI will leave you with roughly the same amount of money at the end of the year. Therefore, I would argue that if you knew with perfect foresight that the behavior of the investment would be similar to price-path B, it would not matter to you whether you used DCA or LSI. Certainly, there would be no particular benefit to DCA, unless the price-path were to wander up and down a great deal on the journey from $100 to $100, in which case DCA would be slightly better, on average.

But when the price stays relatively constant throughout the year, and there is no high and low to speak of, both strategies leave you with roughly the same amount of money. Buying all your caviar at the beginning of the year isn't any worse or better than buying equal dollar amounts of caviar, when the price of caviar doesn't fluctuate. (Of course, if you could predict price-path B, you probably wouldn't bother with this investment to begin with.)

But what if the price-path follows a route similar to C in Figure 2.1? Here, the unit value starts at $100, but drifts steadily lower, losing a substantial sum of money, and finally ends the year at $75 per unit. What if you had perfect foresight, and you knew the investment would lose money? Which strategy would you rather follow? Neither, of course; if you knew the value would drop, you'd keep the money in the bank or invest it elsewhere.

But here, a good case can be made for DCA, as opposed to LSI. That's because if you had taken the plunge right at the beginning of the year and had bought all your units at $100, you'd have suffered a loss of $25 for each and every unit. Using dollar-cost averaging, on the other hand, you would have spread your purchases across the year, during which time the cost per unit was declining, and you would therefore have acquired most of the units at a lower price. Although this may not be much comfort in a declining market, the steady drop in value means that, using DCA, you would not have lost as much when the unit price fell to $75 at the end of the year.

So I must admit, following price-path C, the DCA strategy seems the better of the two investment options.

Okay. But what about price-path A? What if you have perfect foresight and just know that the unit value of the XYZ fund will increase from $100 to $125 by the end of the year? With this premonition, would you rather go the DCA or the LSI route? Would you rather buy slowly, or acquire all your units right away? The obvious answer is that the time to invest is when you have the money — buy in as soon as possible.

If you knew ahead of time that the unit price would rise over the year, you wouldn't wait to invest. Because if you did, you'd be buying at increasingly higher prices. So here, the DCA approach isn't so impressive. If you adopted it in connection with price-path A, you'd have far fewer units and much less money at the end of the year, compared to LSI.

So let's summarize these three cases. With path B, you're indifferent; with path C, you prefer dollar-cost averaging; and with path A, you prefer lump-sum investing.

So is it a tie?

No. In fact, this is precisely where the odds come in. As discussed in later chapters in this book, in the very long run, equity-based investments will increase in value. In other words, in the long run, path A is more likely to occur than either path B or path C. Therefore, since A has the highest odds of occurring — and lump-sum investing is clearly the best choice for that scenario — I must conclude that lump-sum investing gives you the better odds.

Of course, there is no denying the existence of bear markets. In any particular year, there's a strong chance that the final price of XYZ units will be described by path B (flat) or, even worse, path C (downward). But once again, I appeal to the odds of regret. What are the odds that you will regret the decision to dollar-cost average, relative to lump-sum investing? If path A is more likely to occur than path C — and more than two centuries of American capital market history certainly confirm this — then we must conclude that the odds of regret are lower with a lump-sum investment strategy.

If you dollar-cost average, and price-path A is the norm, then you will suffer an investment penalty. The penalty comes from not being in the market from the beginning of the year.

Remember, though, that short-term money does not belong in the stock market, with or without dollar-cost averaging. So if you are planning a long-term investment, and you want the money to end up in fund XYZ, I would advise you to adopt the lump-sum approach, and forget the hype about DCA. And I would recommend this strategy despite the possibility of a devastating market collapse immediately after your single lump-sum investment.

Now, even if you're in it for the long haul, you may still feel uncomfortable about price volatility and fluctuations. Believing that price-path A is more likely doesn't necessarily mean you can forget about risk. Wouldn't dollar-cost averaging help cope with price fluctuations? Wouldn't it mitigate some of the volatility? Maybe, just maybe (you reason), the reduced fluctuations are worth the performance penalty you pay in lower returns. In fact, volatility reduction is the primary justification and rationale for portfolio diversification. You sacrifice some returns, but you sleep better knowing that your investment is less prone to unexpected tremors — to volatility.

It's an interesting argument. And, to be fair, it's a valid one. But in my judgment — and this is the key — the reduction in your return under dollar-cost averaging is more than it should be for the amount of volatility reduction it offers.

What I am arguing is that there are far more efficient ways to reduce volatility — such as diversifying your capital across stocks and money market funds — without incurring the same penalty imposed by dollar-cost averaging. In other words, if the volatility of a lump-sum strategy concerns you, then my advice is to avoid the stock market to begin with. Or, if you're determined to be in the markets, put 56% of your capital into equities (or equity mutual funds) and put the remaining 44% in a lower-risk money market account. This 56/44 mix will yield the same benefits as dollar-cost averaging — i.e., it will reduce your investment volatility and possibility of loss because only 56% is exposed to the more volatile equity market — without incurring as large a performance penalty.

Figure 2.2 provides a graphical illustration of the problem with dollar-cost averaging. The horizontal axis displays the volatility or uncertainty in the outcome of the investment strategy, while the vertical axis displays your expected long-term return. The higher you are on the ver-

Figure 2.2 The Investment Trade-off

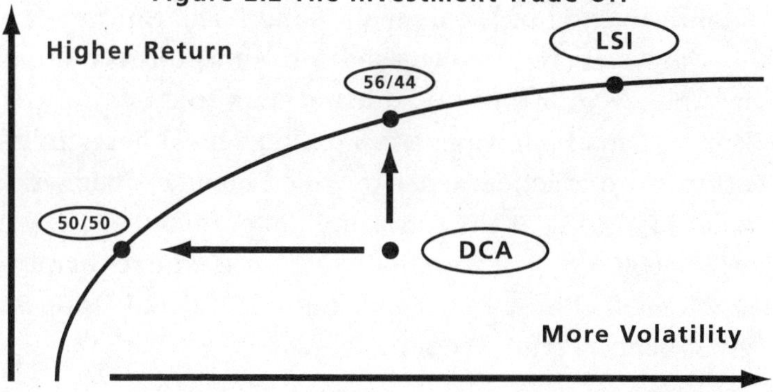

tical axis, the higher is your expected return. Likewise, the further you are to the right on the horizontal axis, the higher the volatility or uncertainty associated with the strategy.

As you can see, lump-sum investing (in the upper right-hand corner) provides you with a greater expected return than dollar-cost averaging, but it is more volatile or uncertain. Things can go very well or they can turn very sour. In the same picture, you will notice that dollar-cost averaging has a lower volatility and a corresponding lower expected long-term return. Your return is lower because you are not completely invested in the market at all times, but, by the same token, your volatility is lower.

As an alternative to dollar-cost averaging, I propose a 56/44 mix between the equity fund and the money market fund. The result will be a higher level of expected return, with the same level of volatility. Alternatively, an equally valid strategy is to invest with a 50/50 mix between equity and money market funds. The level of expected return will remain the same, but the volatility will be reduced to a level even lower than that realized under DCA.

It is my opinion that investors who enter the market using dollar-cost averaging to mitigate volatility — and planning to be fully invested by year-end — are exhibiting contradictory behavior. On the one hand, they want 100% exposure to the market over the long term; on the other hand, they claim to be concerned with short-term volatility. I say: Choose your time horizon and stick to it.

But perhaps I am waxing too philosophical here. To get a better, more practical sense of what I mean by "reduction in volatility," look at the following table. Imagine that you have $10,000 that you want to invest for the next year, and that you must choose between a mutual fund and a safe 5%-interest-bearing bank account.

Table 2.1

The Effect of Asset Allocation on Returns and Volatility

Amount Allocated to Mutual Fund*	What to Expect at Year-End	Investment's Variability
$10,000	$11,250	(+/–) $2,000
$7,500	$11,062	(+/–) $1,500
$5,600	$10,920	(+/–) $1,121
$5,000	$10,875	(+/–) $1,000
$2,500	$10,688	(+/–) $500
$0	$10,500	(+/–) $0
DCA	$10,875	(+/–) $1,121

**Note: The remaining funds are invested at 5%.*

The fund is expected to earn 12.5% but, in any year, the return can fluctuate by 20% on either side of that figure.

Here's how to read the table. If you invest the entire $10,000 in the mutual fund, at year-end you can expect — no guarantees, mind you — to have $11,250. This is because the mutual fund is expected to appreciate by 12.5% per year. That $1,250, added to your $10,000 investment, will give you $11,250.

However — and this is crucial — mutual fund investment returns are variable. That means that at year-end your final return will be roughly $11,250, plus or minus $2,000. The $2,000 corresponds with the 20% volatility of the mutual fund. So, therefore, in all likelihood (actually two-thirds of the time, according to the laws of statistics), you will have somewhere between $9,250 and $13,250 at the end of the year. But I repeat that you can expect $11,250, which is the midpoint of this spread.

In the same manner, you might expect tomorrow's weather to be 65 degrees Fahrenheit, but the variation can be plus or minus 10 degrees, for example. Therefore, in all likelihood the temperature will be in the 55–75-degree range.

Let's look at another case in the table. If you allocate nothing to the mutual fund, and put the entire $10,000 into the bank account, you can expect $10,500 at the end of the year — with no variability. This is simply the 5% interest rate, guaranteed.

Now what happens if you put the money in the bank and gradually, using the dollar-cost averaging approach, invest your $10,000 in the mutual fund on a monthly basis? In other words, what can you expect at year-end?

Well, the table indicates that you can expect to have $10,875 at year-end, but with a variability of plus or minus $1,121. So with a DCA strategy, in all likelihood (two-thirds of the time), you will receive between $9,754 and $11,996.

This is where the inefficiency of dollar-cost averaging should become evident. You can see from the table that if you immediately allocate $5,000 to the mutual fund and the remainder to the bank account, you can expect to receive the same $10,875 that a $10,000 DCA investment would yield. But the variability of your investment would be lower at year-end. The variability of the $5,000-in-fund and $5,000-in-bank scenario is plus or minus $1,000, while the variability of DCA is plus or minus $1,121.

What this tells us is that you can generate the same expected return provided by dollar-cost averaging (namely, the $10,875), but with lower variability (and therefore lower risk), by simply splitting your money in half. One part goes into the mutual fund; the other goes into the bank account. At year-end, you will have the same amount, on average, as you would have had with DCA, but your level of uncertainty is reduced.

In the same manner — and from a different angle — the table indicates that if you were to invest $5,600 into the mutual fund, you would have $10,920 at year-end, with a variability of plus or minus $1,121. This, of course, is the same level of variability that dollar-cost averaging would have created. But it provides a better return; here you can expect to earn $45 more than you would have received from DCA ($10,920 – $10,875).

This is why Figure 2.2 has two suggested alternative strategies to dollar-cost averaging: both are more efficient. One strategy (50% in equities, 50% in the bank) gives you lower variability or uncertainty for the same return that DCA would provide; the other (56% in equities, 44% in the bank) gives you greater return — in this case, $45 more — than a DCA approach, with the same amount of variability. It's also administratively simpler, which could mean a saving of time and possibly money.

Now, it may be that you don't regard the $45 difference in return as significant. You might be asking, "If all I stand to lose from using dollar-cost averaging is $45 on a $10,000 investment, who cares?"

I can't argue with that. But remember my original agenda. I simply wanted to convince you that there was and is nothing special or magical about dollar-cost averaging. My main point is that you can do just as well — even slightly better — by not dollar-cost averaging. And that's exactly what this table shows. If you're interested in more of the theory, a great deal of research has been done by economists criticizing and lamenting what they call the fallacy of dollar-cost averaging (see the Notes section for some references).

One of those studies demonstrated quite clearly that over the last 50 years, a dollar-cost averaging investment strategy would have yielded a worse return than a lump-sum investment strategy with the same level of risk. The researchers identified a long-term performance penalty suffered by dollar-cost averaging, which they estimated at between 1% and 4%, depending on the time period and market involved.

Of course, this fact should come as no great surprise, because the markets have trended upwards — price-path A, remember, was the norm. Consequently, the sooner you get in, the better you fare in the long run. For that matter, discovering the occasional period in history when dollar-cost averaging outperformed lump-sum investing is not exactly proof of its superiority; that's like searching out bear markets and declaring that, for that period, money would have done better under the mattress.

In sum, if you feel comfortable investing in a way that will lead to an eventual 100% allocation to equity — what DCA would accomplish by the end of the year anyway — then I recommend that you create that allocation now. Don't procrastinate. If, on the other hand, you're concerned about the volatility that lump-sum investing will involve, then — right now — allocate 56% to equity and 44% to a money market fund and re-evaluate at year-end. Because even that strategy, in my judgment, is better than the piecemeal, 12-segment, DCA approach.

In fact, if you don't have the capital right now, but you plan to automatically withdraw money each month from your paycheck, I'd recommend that you borrow 12 times that amount, pay it back in monthly installments, and create your desired asset allocation right now. Of course, I'm certainly not suggesting that people borrow on their credit cards at 21% interest in order to implement a lump-sum investing strategy. But if the interest rate you pay on borrowing is relatively close to what you would earn on your investments, then by all means, borrow against your future wages and invest in one lump sum.

If you have a long-term investment horizon, and are not particularly disturbed by daily fluctuations, go for the total LSI strategy. If the volatility concerns you, pick the 56/44 solution, or some variation thereof. But whatever you do, do it now.

You may have noticed that new versions of dollar-cost averaging have recently been advocated. These entail investing more than $250 — our hypothetical monthly segment — when the unit price has declined since the previous month, and less than $250 when the unit price has increased. The rationale behind this twist is that when something is on sale, you should buy even more than you originally intended, and when things are pricey, you should buy less. (Of course, go figure when things are relatively cheap or expensive!)

But I find this new wrinkle to be just another form of market timing, which is ill-advised for ordinary, small investors, and mostly a loser's game for professionals. Those who can produce evidence of periods in which a particular strategy (this enhanced-DCA, for example) would have worked are probably not telling you about the thousands of other strategies they examined that did not work. Nor can they promise that this one strategy will continue to prevail.

This is known as the "data mining" problem in financial markets. Analysts have access to thousands of days of historical trading data, which they test against hundreds of different trading strategies, hoping to find one that will outperform the market. Indeed, one or two have been found to work well in the past, but these are simply statistical aberrations with no guarantee of persistence. Among the more humorous is the one that claims that in the year when a team from the National Football League's NFC wins the Super Bowl, stock markets in the U.S. will move up; the reverse will occur if a team from the AFC wins.

Needless to say, my comments about DCA apply equally to these aberrations as well. The painful thing about this enhanced-DCA strategy is that it deprives dollar-cost averaging of the only unquestionable merit it has — namely, the no-brainer, automatic forced saving that its discipline imposes.

CONCLUSION

I believe that institutionalized dollar-cost averaging is a highly commendable financial counseling strategy because it automatically forces people to save for their long-term goals. Indeed, if they had to rely on their own will power — to save whatever is left over after all the monthly bills are paid — many people would fall short of their financial objectives.

From a psychological point of view, dollar-cost averaging may reduce some of the emotional pain that comes with investing the day before the market crashes. But the odds of this happening are remote. More importantly, one must realize that from a conceptual perspective, dollar-cost averaging is simply an inefficient financial strategy. If you have a lump sum of money that you eventually would like to invest completely in the stock market, you are far better off investing it all right now — what I call taking the plunge — as opposed to going the piecemeal DCA route. Replacing one major gamble (the lump sum) with many smaller gambles (DCA) does not make prudent financial sense. As I argued in the numerical example, the process of dollar-cost averaging will destroy $45 of value for every $1,000 you are investing.

Ah, but what if the market falls right after you've taken

the plunge? Well, if you're not comfortable with that prospect, if the market's volatility scares you, or if you fear the dramatic short-term possibility of loss, then you're probably not psychologically suited for total equity exposure. And if that's the case, then from a risk-and-return perspective, you would do well to partition your wealth — right now — between stocks and less volatile financial instruments, and holding both for the long term.

In sum, those who hesitate, lose. The odds are you will do better financially by avoiding dollar-cost averaging. But please don't forget to eat well and exercise regularly!

CHAPTER

3

Home-Cooked Portfolio Insurance:

Can You Invest Your Cake and Eat It Too?

In the 1980s a new breed of financial products was created — one that allowed you to invest in the upward participation of the stock market without the downside risks associated with fluctuating stock prices. These products are collectively known as index-linked notes (ILN) and are still quite popular today. They are called "notes" because, like traditional short-term notes or certificates of deposit, they guarantee to return your original principal at maturity. On the other hand, unlike regular notes or CDs, the investment returns are not provided in the form of regular coupon (interest) payments; rather, they are linked to the performance of a particular stock market index.

To illustrate, let's say that on January 15, 2000, you invested $10,000 in an ordinary two-year (compounding)

CD paying 5% per annum. This means that on January 15, 2002, you would receive your original $10,000 principal, together with $1,025; that corresponds to the 5% interest rate, compounded for two years.

If this were a non-compounding CD, your account would be credited with two separate payments of $500 on January 15, 2001, and January 15, 2002. The net return may seem small. It may even be small, relative to other possible investments. But the important thing — and the defining feature of a conventional CD — is that you know right from the start exactly "what you're going to get."

In rather sharp contrast, with an indexed-linked note you do not know "what you're going to get" until the date of maturity. The interest rate will be determined only when the contract expires. Moreover, the actual interest rate will depend in part on how the stock market index performs — hence the name "index-linked." The higher the stock market index goes during the life of your ILN, the higher your return.

But what if the stock market idles in neutral over the life of your certificate? Worse, what if it crashes? In that case, your investment will earn zero interest. That's the bad news.

The good news is that your original principal is guaranteed. Even if the stock market index were to collapse, the worst that could happen is that you'd get all of your money back at maturity.

Now, the actual relationship between the performance of the stock market index and the interest rate credited to your account depends on a formula. At times that formula can be quite complicated. The important thing to remember here is that the interest rate payable on an index-linked note is unknown until the certificate matures. Of course, you can get a good estimate of your probable return by monitoring the overall performance of the stock market index over the life of the index-linked note.

There are other complexities to consider as well. Many different types of index-linked note are available from your broker. The differences depend on

- the length or maturity date of the note;
- the exact formula used to calculate the interest rate; and
- the stock market to which the product is linked.

So, in some sense, index-linked notes allow you to have your investment cake and eat it too. Of course, the astute reader will notice some caveats associated with these products:

1. The underlying index from which your return is computed *usually* does not include dividends. Whatever dividends the stocks that make up the index generate during the life of your contract will not accrue to you.

2. If the market declines, your principal capital will be returned in full at maturity. But in the meantime, you will have lost the potential interest income that could have been obtained from a conventional term deposit, CD, or regular note. Economists refer to this as the "lost opportunity" cost.

3. In many cases, the formula for computing the return on the index-linked note is capped at a fixed annual percentage rate. If the returns on the underlying index, net of dividends, are greater than the capped rate, you do not participate in any further upward movement.

So, as you can see, the downside protection does not come free. You have to pay for it with forfeited interest, dividends, and potential growth. On the other hand, the concept of downside protection may appeal to you, despite the imputed costs.

Therefore, the subject I will explore in this chapter is the question of how you can invest directly in the stock market and create or "cook" your own downside protection at home, without buying any of the above products sold by financial institutions.

You can effectively manufacture your own safeguarded investment — $10,000, say — by buying, for the same total price, (1) financial products that provide the potential for stock market growth and (2) financial products that replicate the downside protection. At the same time, you have the freedom to build in some flexibility.

I should note at the outset that although these strategies will reduce your odds of regret, their implementation can be somewhat complicated; they are, therefore, not for everybody. In fact, if you're a novice investor, you might want to skip this chapter on first reading, and come back to it at a later time. And please bear in mind that if you do decide to cook at home, you will need a standard brokerage account and possibly the help of an investment adviser licensed to sell options.

With that preamble, I'd now like to show you two alternative ways to replicate a two-year, $10,000, S&P 500 index–linked note (ILN) with a 20% growth cap. You will have to trust me that alternative indices, maturities, and payout structures can be handled in a similar fashion.

Let's deal first with the downside protection. We know that regular ILNs build in downside protection — in two years, you are guaranteed to receive $10,000. But the same downside protection can be created by purchasing something called a zero-coupon bond.

A zero-coupon (government) bond is a bond with no coupons or interest payments attached. Unlike a regular bond, which entitles you to semi-annual coupons, a zero-coupon bond will provide you with absolutely no interest payments over its life. At maturity, all you will get is the face value of the bond, which can be $1,000, $10,000, or even $100,000. These products are also known as STRIPS, which stands for Separate Trading of Registered Interest and Principal of Securities.

Wait a minute, you say. No coupons? No interest payments? Why would I ever buy such a bond from the government? Don't I pay enough in taxes?

Well, here's the point, subtle though it may be. Although zero-coupon bonds give you no interest payments along the way, you will get implicit interest payments at maturity. That's because zero-coupon bonds always sell for less than face value. In other words, you will always pay less than $1,000, $10,000, or $100,000 for the bond that matures at $1,000, $10,000, or $100,000. Because you are paying less than its maturity value, you are earning (as de facto interest compensation) the difference between the purchase price and the maturity value.

For example, at the time of writing you could pay $9,000 to buy a U.S. government zero-coupon bond that is guaranteed to mature at $10,000 in two years. The guaranteed gain from this transaction is $1,000 and represents an interest rate of $1,000/$9,000 = 11.1% for two years, or a compounded 5.4% per year.

Essentially, a zero-coupon bond functions like a compounded term deposit, where the interest is implicitly re-invested. You can buy zero-coupon bonds with maturities that stretch out as far as 25 or even 30 years. Again, there will be no interest payments for 25 years, but the waiting will pay off at maturity.

At the same time, you can buy a 25-year zero-coupon bond for $2,600, which is guaranteed to mature at $10,000 in 25 years. Sounds impressive, doesn't it? You pay just

$2,600 and get $10,000 back. Is there some sort of catch? Is this a pyramid scheme? Not at all. Remember, you won't be getting any money back for 25 years, so the compensation must be large. Here, in this instance, the guaranteed gain is $7,400 and represents a compound interest rate of approximately 5.5% for the next 25 years. Very safe, but hardly spectacular.

That the bonds don't mature for 25 years doesn't mean you can't sell them for 25 years. In fact, you can probably sell them at any time of day or night by calling your broker, who probably bought them for you in the first place, and by placing an order to sell. Of course, you won't get the full $10,000 — for that you must wait until maturity. But more likely than not, you'll get more than you paid.

Unfortunately, the tax treatment of these zero-coupon bonds can get messy, if they are held outside a tax-sheltered plan such as a 401(k), 403(b), or IRA. When you buy a zero-coupon bond, the IRS considers you to have implicitly received interest each and every year you hold the bond, even though you don't actually get your money until maturity (or when you sell it).

The reason I'm going on about these zero-coupon bonds is that they are a perfect way to guarantee a lump sum of money at some point in the future. For example, if you want to make sure that you have exactly $10,000 in exactly 10 years, you can buy a zero-coupon bond today for about $5,800, hold the bond for a decade (i.e., until maturity), and then get the $10,000 from (and backed by) the U.S. government.

Notice, however, that you only need about $5,800 today to get $10,000 at maturity. You obviously don't need the full $10,000. The important thing to remember is that if you have $10,000 that you want to invest in the stock market for 10 years, but you want downside protection on the capital, you can get it with zero-coupon bonds. So, if you set aside $5,800 — by buying zero-coupon bonds that mature at $10,000 — you can then use the remaining $4,200 to invest in the stock market. Even if you were to lose the entire $4,200 (not terribly likely), you are still guaranteed to receive the $10,000 bond payment in 10 years.

Now, let's return to our two-year ILN example. To cook one yourself, you're going to buy a zero-coupon bond for $9,000, guaranteed to mature at $10,000 in two years. Again, the guaranteed gain from this transaction is $1,000 and represents an interest rate of $1,000/$9,000 = 11.1% for two years, or a compound 5.4% for one year.

But what about the upside potential of ILN? How can that be replicated at home? The answer involves the use of financial instruments known as options.

Options are traded, listed, bought, and sold on an options exchange, which is usually located right next door to a stock exchange. Chicago and New York have large option markets. There are two basic types of options — calls and puts.

A call option is a contract that gives you the right, but not the obligation, to buy shares of an underlying stock at a pre-specified fixed price. For example, if you buy a contract of 100 IBM call options, you then have the right, but not the obligation, to buy 100 shares of IBM stock at a predetermined price during a pre-specified period of time.

To be more specific, you can pay $400 now to purchase the right, but not the obligation, to pay another $3,000 to acquire 100 shares of IBM sometime over the next six months. In this example, the $400 is called the option premium and the $30 (times 100) is usually referred to as the strike price. If the price of 100 shares goes above $3,000 in the next six months, you would want to exercise your call option; at that point, you can hold on to the shares, or you can turn around and sell the shares right away for a quick return. On the other hand, if the price of 100 shares stays the same or goes down in the next six months, you will "strike out" or lose on the original investment.

Obviously, you will only exercise the call option when the price of 100 shares of IBM is above the strike price of $3,000. After all, why would you pay more than it was worth? When the value is above the strike price, it is called "being in the money."

So there are two prices (or numbers) to monitor: the price at which you purchase the 100 IBM call options (the $400 premium), and the price at which the options allow you to purchase 100 shares of IBM (the $30 per share). These two numbers, however, represent very different things.

In fact, there is nothing special about the $30 (per share) strike price; it could have been higher — $35 for example — or lower ($25). If you think about it for a minute, you will agree that the lower the strike price at which the call option contract allows you to buy IBM, the more you must pay for this right. In other words, the lower the strike price, the higher the premium. Indeed, it's not uncommon to see four to eight different call options trading on a stock like IBM, each with its own strike price. For example, you might see the $25 (per share) strike price selling for $7 (per share), and the $35 strike price selling for $2 (per share).

Here's another term we will need to understand: an "out-of-the-money" call. An out-of-the-money call is a call option with a strike price that is above the current price of the underlying stock when the call is purchased. For example, if IBM is trading at $30 per share, a call option with a strike price of $36 per share would be 20% out-of-the-money (the $6 differential being one-fifth, or 20%, of the current trading price). A call option with a strike price of $33 per share would be 10% out-of-the-money. A call option with a strike price of exactly $30 per share is said to be "at-the-money."

Why, you reasonably ask, would anyone buy an out-of-the-money call option? Well, remember that the higher the strike price, the lower the premium. For a $36 strike price on one share of IBM, your premium might only be $1.50 per share. If you had a clear expectation that the value of IBM shares would rise over the time-frame of your option, then this strategy might make very good sense.

Now let's take a look at put options.

A put option is the exact opposite of a call option. A put is a contract that gives you the right, but not the obligation, to sell shares of the underlying stock at a fixed price over a pre-specified period. Thus, if you buy a put on IBM, you have the right, but not the obligation, to sell 100 shares of IBM stock during a particular window of time and at a certain price.

For example, you can pay $350 now to purchase the right, but not the obligation, to sell 100 shares of IBM at $3,000, sometime over the next six months. Once again, the $350 is called the put option premium; the $30 (per share) is referred to as the put option strike price. In the puts case, if the price of 100 shares of IBM does not fall below $3,000 in the next six months, you will "strike out," or lose on the original investment. Put options are the stock market equivalent of car insurance. When you insure your $20,000 car, you have essentially acquired the right (but definitely not the obligation) to demolish your car and then sell it back to the insurance company for $20,000. Some people choose a $1,000 deductible, so the strike price is only $19,000, which leads to lower premiums.

You do not need to own shares of a particular stock in order to buy an option. In fact, just like a regular stock, the options exchange lets you buy and sell puts and calls anytime over the life of the option. Thus, you can make (or lose) money without ever having to buy or sell the underlying stock.

In addition to options on individual stocks, you can also

buy and sell puts and calls on gold, silver, foreign currencies, stock indices, and even commodities like pork bellies and heating oil. Bought and sold on an options exchange, these options give you the right, but not the obligation, to buy (with a call) and/or sell (with a put) a fixed quantity of the underlying security at a fixed price.

Why the long lecture on options?

Well, it's safe to assume that financial institutions "hedge" every index-linked note they sell to the public using the same financial instruments I've just been describing. In other words, these institutions are financially engineering the product. For an index-linked note with a 20% growth cap, for example, they probably take a portion of your deposit, buy a zero-coupon bond (for downside protection), sell 20% out-of-the-money calls, and buy at-the-money calls. And my argument simply is that if the banks, trust companies, and credit unions can do it, so can you.

We've already seen how you can create your own downside protection, or guarantee, by paying $9,000 to buy two-year zero-coupon bonds that will mature at $10,000. Now you can use the remaining $1,000 to get the call options you need to replicate the upside potential of an ILN.

Specifically, you will need to purchase two-year at-the-money call options on about $10,000 worth of S&P 500 index stock and sell an equal number of two-year 20% out-of-the-money call options on the same stock. This, and only this, combination will create the upward participation you need — but with the 20% cap — just like the index-linked note. You could choose a different underlying index or stock, as long as it is highly correlated with the index linked to the ILN you're interested in mimicking.

Why buy the two-year at-the-money call options? Because at maturity, if the price of the S&P 500 index has gone up, you can exercise those call options to realize a profit equal to the difference between the new maturity price and your at-the-money strike price. This represents your upward participation.

And of course, you sell two-year 20% out-of-the-money call options to generate income now, from the premium. (Remember that you can buy and sell call options — which are essentially obligations, or promises — without actually owning anything.)

If, at maturity, the S&P 500 stock price goes above 20%, here's what will happen: the buyer of your call options will gleefully exercise the call, so you will owe him or her the difference between (a) the high, maturity-date stock price and (b) 120% of the underlying stock price at the date you sold the options.

In other words, your at-the-money call has fully exposed you to the gains in the stock price, but your obligations from the sale of out-of-the-money call options mean that you have to pay someone else the proceeds beyond 20%. This represents your 20% growth cap.

A broker can give you the precise numbers but, roughly speaking, the at-the-money call would (at the time of writing) cost you $1,500, while selling the out-of-the-money calls would net you $500. Do the math and you are left with a bill of $1,000 for the options, which you pay with the $1,000 left over from the purchase of the zero-coupon bond.

In reality, the option prices would fluctuate hourly — and your results may be slightly different from those described above — but hopefully the central idea is clear.

The numbers in our example are also somewhat biased in that we did not include any brokerage fees or transaction costs. When you take brokerage fees into account, you may earn less than $500 from selling the 20% out-of-the-money call option. And you may have to pay more than $1,500 for the at-the-money call option. But my goal here is to give you a general sense of how this strategy would work — not to give you precise numbers for your profit and loss.

In fact, I'm pretty certain that for sums of money less than $10,000, the commissions, transaction costs, and fees attached to trying to replicate the product at home can be prohibitive. The providers of index-linked notes (buying wholesale versus buying retail) use their economies of scale to purchase these "options" at a better overall price than you, as a small investor, could ever hope to obtain.

However, for sums greater than $10,000, you can probably cook this recipe — or a very similar product — at home for less.

Now, as you may recall, I mentioned earlier that there were two distinct ways to create your own investment with downside protection and growth potential. Here is another strategy that may be even better than the zero-coupon-plus-call-option combination.

Perhaps a simpler alternative to buying a generic S&P 500 index–linked note is to purchase Spiders, which are traded on the American Stock Exchange, together with some put options for protection.

What are Spiders?

Spiders is an acronym for S&P 500 Depository Receipts. They are very similar in structure and purpose to an equity mutual fund, with a few key differences. First, this mutual fund always has 500 stocks in it — no more, no less. These 500 stocks are among the largest capitalization stocks traded in the U.S. The Standard and Poor's committee decides which stocks go in and out, but there is no fund manager checking the market daily, deciding what and when to buy and sell. This makes Spiders much cheaper to manage, compared with regular mutual funds.

Second, like closed-end mutual funds and stocks, Spiders are actually traded on a stock exchange, so you can buy and sell these units at any time during the trading day. However, the American Stock Exchange has structured the product so that the problems usually associated with exchange-traded funds have been eliminated. For example, large institutions can create or redeem Spiders at the net asset value (NAV); in other words, they can exchange the units for the underlying stocks. Also, cash dividends are collected from the companies in the index and then distributed to unit-holders each and every quarter, minus a management fee of 19 basis points (which is 0.19%) per year. This makes Spiders one of the cheapest methods for investing in the stock market.

Here's a simplified example of how you can use Spiders to create an investment with both growth potential and downside protection. Say you have $10,000 to invest for two years. You want to expose yourself to some upside market potential, but want to avoid the downside risk. You check the newspaper's business section and find that each Spiders (symbol SPY) unit sells for $35. Note: Normally, they are quoted at one-tenth the value of the underlying S&P 500 index.

So you buy 285 Spiders for a total cost of $10,000. That takes care of the potential upside. If the price of each Spider rises to $40 in two years, you'll have made $1,425 (285 x $5). And in the meantime, you are entitled to receive full quarterly dividends, to pay capital gains taxes only upon disposition of the shares, and to enjoy complete liquidity, i.e., the ability to sell at any time.

But what about the downside? To protect your investment, you could decide to buy put options on the S&P 500 *index*. Remember, the equity put option is like an insurance contract that protects your principal for the life of the option. In this case, you could buy 285 units of two-year puts, each with a strike price of $35, and a market premium of $3.16 — which is quoted from a broker — for a total cost of approximately $900 (285 x $3.16). That means that if the unit price of Spiders falls to $30 or even to $25 during that year, you still have the option to sell your Spiders for your original $35 per unit. (Once again, please remember that these prices tend to fluctuate hourly.) If the price of Spiders goes up, you won't exercise your puts — but since your Spiders are doing well, you're happy.

Of course, to buy those "protective puts," you would have to spend an additional $900. That's fair, given the insurance they provide. But what if you don't want to commit an additional $900 to protect your $10,000? In fact, doesn't an index-linked note protect your $10,000 without requiring any more money?

Well, there is a way to protect the $10,000 you've invested in the stock market — without dishing out an additional $900 for the puts. The way to do this is by giving up some of your rights. Specifically, you would have to relinquish your right to any appreciation above 20% and essentially forfeit your right to any dividends.

Here's how you might do this. You would finance part of the puts purchase (and lose your yield above 20%) by selling 285 units of 20% out-of-the-money call options. This is the same strategy used in the zero-coupon-plus-calls scenario to finance the protective at-the-money calls. An out-of-the-money call, you'll remember, is a call option with a strike price that is above the current price of the underlying stock. If our strike price in this example is $35, the strike price of the call option will be $42 (120% of $35). You will get a premium for selling these calls, but if the price of Spiders goes above $42 at the end of your two years, the buyer is going to exercise the option, and you'll have to pay them the difference (anything over 20%). This "skimming" effect is your 20% growth cap.

In current market conditions — according to broker quotes — selling these 285 units of 20% out-of-the-money calls would give you about $500 (285 x the premium price of $1.75). So you now have to finance only $400 ($900 – $500) to buy the protective puts. But with a bit of luck, you can expect to receive $400 worth of dividends from the 285 Spiders that you are holding outright.

So what do you have when the day is over? You have 285 units of Spiders, plus 285 put options, struck at $35 to protect those Spiders. And you have sold 285 call options with a strike price of $42 to finance part of the put purchase. The dividends from the Spiders should, it is hoped, finance the rest, which is why I said you are giving up the dividends. You are giving them up as they arrive — to pay for the original puts.

Is this Spiders-plus-puts combination simpler than the zero-coupon strategy?

In some ways, yes. It's a bit easier to understand, and it comes with a more preferential tax treatment, because you essentially own equity investments that entitle you to capital gains.

So there you have it. I have demonstrated two ways to create a two-year investment in the S&P 500 index, with complete downside protection, but with a growth cap of 20%.

As I suggested, the self-constructed strategy is not for everybody. Certainly, unless you're a very sophisticated investor, you wouldn't want to cook it without the help of a trusted adviser.

CONCLUSION

The possibility of financial regret drives many consumers to acquire investment products that provide upside potential together with downside protection. The purpose of this chapter was to show that downside investment protection can be obtained independently using equity and index options known as puts and calls; in other words, there's nothing magic about the ILNs offered by financial institutions. If you understand how the product is constructed (or replicated), then you are in a better position to determine whether or not you would like to own one. And if you do decide to "cook at home," you may be able to create an investment that is more flexible than any of the standard products available in the marketplace.

Of course, the real cost of the do-it-yourself approach is the time, effort, and complexity that these strategies entail. And only you can decide whether the potential savings and benefits justify those costs.

CHAPTER

4

Variable Annuities:

An Investment to Die For?

At first glance, a variable annuity (VA) and a mutual fund are quite similar investment products. You can buy both VAs and mutual funds from your favorite investment broker, financial adviser, or even through your local bank. For the most part, they are both designed and intended as long-term savings vehicles, administered by professional money managers who attempt to earn the highest investment returns — while keeping risk to a minimum — using stocks and bonds and a variety of other money market instruments. Variable annuities and mutual funds can be purchased in small amounts, on either a one-time or a regular basis, and are fairly liquid as well as cashable.

Of course, these money management services do not come free, and the investor in a mutual fund or variable annuity must pay annual fees. Unlike your lawyer or accountant, VA and mutual fund managers don't send you an annual bill for their services, but rather deduct a proportional fee directly from your investment account. Nevertheless, Americans have embraced VAs and mutual funds to save and build wealth for their golden retirement years; as of January 2000, Americans had approximately $680 billion invested in variable annuities and $2.8 trillion invested in mutual funds, according to Morningstar Inc. in Chicago.

But general similarities aside, there are some very important differences between variable annuities and mutual funds, and this chapter will discuss those distinctions in detail. For example, it is a fact that variable annuities provide some additional tax and insurance benefits that are currently not available with generic mutual funds. And, as a result, the implicit and explicit fees on variable annuities are higher than for mutual funds. However, the main message of this chapter is as follows. *Despite the additional benefits of variable annuities, I would recommend that you invest instead in no-load, low-expense mutual funds.* Analysis of the same type of computer simulations that I discussed in the Introduction — Monte Carlo simulations — indicates that extra fees are not worth the additional benefits. The only exception to my "VA-avoidance rule" would be for people who have completely maxed out all other tax shelters, such as 401(k) and IRA plans, and who are in a high tax bracket right now but expect to be in a very low one during their retirement years. In that case, they may wish to purchase an ultra-low-cost VA product, which is offered by a small group of annuity vendors such as TIAA-CREF, based in New York City, or Vanguard. But for most people, a simple mutual fund would be the best investment option for building wealth for retirement. But let me start from the beginning.

What are the main differences between a variable annuity and a mutual fund?

First of all, variable annuities are manufactured and distributed by insurance companies, while mutual funds are created by investment companies. You will see why in a minute. Second, at the great risk of oversimplifying, I would say that despite the many similarities, there are two main benefits to investing in a variable annuity rather than in a mutual fund. The first is related to income taxes, so I'll call it the Tax Benefit. The other, more obscure, benefit is related to life insurance; this I will call the Death Benefit. Benjamin Franklin once said that "in this world, nothing can be said to be certain, except death and taxes," so let me talk about both of them.

The Tax Benefit

In general, when you invest money in a mutual fund, all realized gains during the year are taxed in the hands of the fund-holder. For example, if you invest $1,000 in a mutual fund, and the fund earns a 10% return during the year, you then have to pay tax on the fraction of the $100 that was realized, or, in other words, distributed directly to you as separate income. If $60 came from the sale of stocks, interest, or dividends, and the other $40 were not realized, then you — the unit-holder — have to pay tax on the $60, right now. Even if you re-invest the $60, which most of us tend to do, you have to pay tax on the realized gains. On the other hand, you won't have to pay tax on the other $40 — the unrealized portion — until sometime in the future when you eventually sell the mutual fund units. The key thing to remember is that realized gains are taxed immediately (more precisely, when you file the tax return the following year), while unrealized gains are taxed once you dispose of the investment, which may not happen for 25 years.

In stark contrast, with variable annuities all gains are considered unrealized, regardless of their source or timing. This is because annuities are formally classified as insurance products (for reasons that will be discussed a little later), which enjoy unique tax treatment. In the above example, if the investment were in a variable annuity instead of a mutual fund, you would not have to pay any taxes on the $100 gain until you sold the variable annuity. Stated differently, the variable annuity mechanism defers all tax liability until the annuity is terminated and withdrawals are made. You can therefore think of a variable annuity as a mutual fund whose gains are tax-deferred until withdrawal. In fact, if you decide to convert your variable annuity into an immediate annuity — which is a form of payout option — you will defer your tax liability even further into the future.

Now, this "tax sheltering" of gains has two obvious benefits. First, you don't have to worry about taxes until you sell your variable annuity. Second, if your tax rate is lower at the time you sell your variable annuity than it was when you first purchased it, you will have the additional benefit of paying taxes — on those many years of investment gains — at a lower rate. Naturally, if you have to pay taxes, you would much rather pay them when your tax rate is lower.

I like to think of a variable annuity as a mutual fund with an IRS-approved time-travel machine. It lets you obtain all the investment gains of a mutual fund, but the IRS considers the gains to have occurred *in the future*, on the day you terminate the variable annuity — rather than when they really occurred, year by year.

Now, before you rush out and buy a variable annuity to defer all your taxes, a few caveats are in order. First, when you do sell your variable annuity, the income is all considered ordinary in nature and is taxed at your employment income's marginal tax bracket. In other words, even though the actual gains may have contained some capital components, they "lose" their capital classification when they travel through the tax-time machine.

This may not seem like a big deal, but think back to the mutual fund without the generous tax deferral. You have to pay tax each and every year on dividends and capital gains distributions, but for the most part you're paying at the capital gains tax rate, which is lower than the ordinary income tax rate. Also, when you actually sell the mutual fund, you will pay taxes on all those years of unrealized gains, but at the capital gains rate as well. So there is a very definite trade-off. With a variable annuity you are pushing your tax liability ahead in time, but the rate you end up paying will be higher than it would be for capital gains.

Another point worth mentioning is that if you decide to collapse your variable annuity prior to age 59.5, the IRS will hit you with a 10% penalty on the earnings in the account. This is in addition to any taxes that will be due at that time. Why the penalty? Well, the point of the variable annuity — and the tax break — is to encourage long-term savings to fund retirement. A 10% penalty will make you think twice before you dip into your VA to fund that snazzy new car.

So far I have mentioned two caveats about a VA's favored tax status. These are tax concerns you should have while living. But there are some tax concerns you should have about death as well. It is a fact that annuities are not "stepped up" in tax basis upon your death. So, for example, if your $10,000 investment in a VA were to be worth $20,000 at the time of your death, your heirs would immediately have to pay tax on the $10,000 gain (except under special circumstances, such as if they immediately converted the inherited VA into a life annuity that carries its own tax protection). This is quite different from a comparable mutual fund investment, which your heirs would inherit without any immediate tax consequences.

But one of the most critical drawbacks with variable annuities is the amount you have to pay the insurance company for the asset management services and insurance charges. The fees tend to be higher than mutual fund fees, by about 0.74% per year. In other words, on a year-by-year basis, the average mutual fund charges 74 basis points less than the average variable annuity. (We will return to the question of why that is in just a moment.) Variable annuities also tend to have larger back-end loads. This means that if you sell your annuity within the first few years of purchase, you will likely be hit with a 5%–8% deferred sales charge, which is distinct from any tax consequences.

In any event, unlike mutual funds, variable annuities contain a tax benefit; they allow investors to build and then consume (in the annuitization stage) gains in a tax-favorable manner. Of course, this benefit does not explain why you should be paying more in annual management fees for a VA, since it costs the insurance company nothing to provide the tax shelter. The U.S. Treasury and Congress are responsible for that. So why else would you consider investing in a VA?

The Death Benefit

Variable annuities also provide a unique death benefit that stipulates that *at least* the original investment will be returned to the estate or beneficiary of the policy, *regardless* of the performance of the underlying assets in the account. You can think of this as a money-back guarantee on your investment.

In other words, even if you, the contract owner, were to die during a bear market, and even if your investment were showing a paper loss, the guarantee applies: your heirs will get back your original capital (also known as the contract "premium").

With some contracts, an "enhanced" death benefit feature is available; this version typically provides for a "step-up" or a "roll-up" of the "floor," or minimum guaranteed death benefit. In a step-up version, for instance, the floor will be stepped up every year (or every five years, or some other interval) to the higher of the amount contributed or the value of the underlying assets in the account at that time. In the roll-up version, the insurance company promises to increase the floor by a set percentage (say, 5%) every year. Also, the floor is usually subject to a cap, such as 200% of the amount contributed. The death benefit typically ends at age 80 or 75, and sometimes as early as age 65.

So, all VA contracts are *not* created equal. Let's examine these different types of variable annuities a little more closely.

Assume that you invested $10,000 in a variable annuity on January 1, 2000. Let us further assume that you astutely allocated the $10,000 among a variety of subaccounts — domestic bonds, foreign stocks, emerging market equities — and that by good fortune, the money grew to $12,000 by January 1, 2001. This is a very respectable 20% return for the first year. But suppose that in the second year, world markets collapse unexpectedly and by January 1, 2002, the market value of your investment falls to $8,000. This is a gut-wrenching –33% return for the year 2001. Then, adding permanent injury to insult, on January 1, 2002, when you get your year-end statement, you suffer a fatal heart attack and move (literally) to greener pastures.

Of course, the variable annuity will not be your heirs' first concern. But what happens to it? Once the shock of your death has been absorbed, what are they left with?

Well, if you bought the basic return-of-premium variety of VA, the insurance company owes your estate $2,000. Why $2,000? Well, the original investment ($10,000) is now worth only $8,000; the investment itself is transferred to your heirs. But the insurance company must fulfill its promise and make up the loss, so it will send a check for $10,000, which is the annuity death benefit per the terms of the contract.

However, if you purchased a roll-up version — a return-of-premium plus 5% interest guarantee, for example — then the insurer would owe your heirs $3,000. Again, the first $2,000 is for the loss, and the additional $1,000 represents the interest — 5% on $10,000 for the two years you held the investment. So your heirs now have $11,000. Technically, of course, the heirs will get one big check for $11,000, and $1,000 of that amount will be taxable as ordinary income.

There is nothing special about 5%; some companies offer a higher guarantee, while others offer a lower number. But it's important to note that most companies cap the total guaranteed gain at 200%. In other words, if you invested $10,000 in a variable annuity with a guaranteed return of 5%, the most you are guaranteed at death is $20,000. Of course, you might get much more than that if the market does well. But if the market tanks, your heirs won't get more than 200% of your original investment.

As noted above, other VA products contain an annual ratchet provision. Thus, if on January 1, 2001, the account is worth $12,000, the guaranteed amount becomes $12,000. And even if in year two the market collapses to $8,000, the insurance company is still obligated to give your heirs at least the amount set at the last ratchet. In this instance, then, it would write your heirs a check for $4,000 + $8,000 = $12,000.

Some products offer annual ratchets; others ratchet every five or even 10 years. Clearly, the more frequently they ratchet the better it is for you, since the highest anniversary amount applies. If markets go up, the guaranteed amount is increased. If markets go down, the last ratchet stands.

Now, if during the year 2001 the market continues its upward path, and your account becomes worth $15,000 on

January 1, 2002, then your heirs would inherit an account worth $15,000. There would be no insurance payment to speak of. In other words, the insurance guarantee kicks in only if the account is showing a loss relative to the established level.

So, you can think of a variable annuity as an investment plus a life insurance policy. For example, in the simple return-of-premium example above, the insurance death benefit was $2,000. The policy is paid for via asset-based insurance fees (not present with regular mutual funds) that are deducted from the account. The death benefit consists of the difference between the guaranteed amount and the account value at death.

Unlike life insurance, which is usually received income-tax-free, the VA death benefit is taxable as ordinary income to the extent that it exceeds the amount invested, as I explained earlier. So it's not a perfect substitute for life insurance. Another difference is that life insurance often requires medical (and financial) underwriting, whereas there is no underwriting for VAs.

Also, in practice, you don't know in advance what the death benefit, if any, will be. That's because you can't know in advance whether the account will be showing a loss when you die.

Nevertheless, you can think of it as a life insurance policy with a random face value. The face value may be large — if you die during a bear market — or the face value may be zero, if you die in a bull market.

The Annuitization Pseudo-Benefit

Insurance companies will be quick to point out another benefit to investing for retirement using VAs. Specifically, all variable annuities, by virtue of their insurance classification, contain the right, but not the obligation, to convert the variable annuity account into a lifelong income that cannot be outlived (an immediate annuity). This conversion process is known as "annuitization," and the rate at which you can make that conversion is referred to as the guaranteed annuitization rate. Now, although I am a fan of annuitization — and we will discuss immediate annuities in greater detail in chapter 8 — I claim that the embedded option to annuitize is not much of a benefit. After all, you can take any money, whether it is in a variable annuity or a mutual fund or even in your favorite piggy bank, and use it to purchase an immediate annuity. So, there is nothing special, or for that matter valuable, about a VA's guaranteed annuitization option. Indeed, the fixed immediate annuity rates that insurance companies guarantee in their contracts are almost always worse than current market rates. So you probably won't use them, even if you do decide to annuitize. Furthermore, current estimates are that fewer than 5% (or even as little as 1%) of variable annuity holders actively choose to annuitize.

So, benefits and phantom benefits aside, now that we understand a little bit better how the unique features of variable annuities work, we are in a position to ask how much you should pay for these added features. But first, let me explain how you pay for these features.

As I mentioned in the introduction to the chapter, the fees on mutual funds and variable annuities are paid by a proportional amount. You might think of this proportional expense ratio as comparable to the markup you pay when buying retail instead of wholesale. For example, if the underlying investments contained in your mutual fund or variable annuity earn 13% over the year, and the total expense ratio is 3%, then you'll be credited with a 10% return. Except for minor timing issues, the difference between the gross return earned by the fund manager, and the net return credited to your account, is the proportional expense ratio.

This proportional expense is very different from an annual service charge of $50 or $100 for the account. The proportional expense ratio is applied to your account balance, so the exact amount of money the company deducts is unknown in advance. If the account does well, the company will take out (the same percentage, but) a higher nominal amount. If, on the other hand, the account does poorly, the company takes out (the same percentage, but) a smaller nominal amount. Of course, the sore point is that the proportional expense ratio is charged year after year, regardless of the actual performance of the underlying fund. On the plus side, you can think of it as an incentive for the money managers to grow your investment at the highest and fastest possible rate, so they can pay themselves more.

As I write this, the average expense ratio on the universe of U.S. mutual funds is about 1.37%; this is a simple average of about 8,200 mutual funds listed by Morningstar Inc. By contrast, the average expense ratio on the universe of variable annuities is about 2.11%; this is an average of the 6,600 variable annuity subaccounts listed by Morningstar Inc. Now, please note that these are averages across a whole range of companies, so you might locate a variable annuity that charges much less than comparable mutual funds (for example, from TIAA-CREF), or you might see variable annuities that charge much more. Regardless, the 0.74% difference in average annual expenses between variable annuities and mutual funds demands an explanation. You would assume that it has something to do with the additional benefits. But are the added benefits of a variable annuity worth the extra 0.74% (or 74 basis points)? An even more pressing question is whether 0.74% is worth worrying about. After all, it is less than 1%.

My answer is that for the most part, the benefits are not worth the extra expense. But, unfortunately, given that these expense ratios seem so small when compared with the month-to-month volatility of the financial markets (which sometimes reaches up to 15%), it is quite difficult to develop an intuitive sense of their long-term detrimental effects.

Well, here is a thought experiment that should help. Think of two investments, Product A and Product B. They both invest in exactly the same securities and are essentially mirror images of each other. But there is one important difference. Product A is run by a non-profit organization that charges a zero expense ratio. Product B is managed by a conventional company and charges a hefty expense ratio. If both funds hold identical securities, then of course their gross annual returns will be the same. Net returns, though, will differ. Product A's net return will be the same as its gross return — because its expense ratio is zero. Product B will suffer from an expense ratio drag. Over time, the gap in cumulative returns will get larger and larger.

(You might think that a zero expense ratio must be a figment of my imagination. In fact, Vanguard — with its 18-basis-point charge on the S&P 500 index fund — is almost there. S&P 500 exchange–traded funds, which are quite similar to mutual funds, also register expense ratios in the low teens.)

Now, assume that you invest $100 in Product B (high expenses), and you plan to hold the fund for 10 years. How much money would you have to invest in Product A (zero expenses), so that you end up with exactly the same amount of money in 10 years? Clearly, you would need to invest less than $100 to catch up to Product B in 10 years. But *how much less*? Table 4.1 provides some answers.

Here's how to read the table. A 150-basis-point annual expense on $100 invested for 20 years amounts to $25.92 in today's dollars. This means that investing $100 in a product

Table 4.1

The Present Value of "Small" Annual Expenses

Assumed holding period for the $100 initial investment

Annual Expense	1 year	5 years	10 years	20 years	30 years
20 basis points	$0.20	$1.00	$1.98	$3.92	$5.82
50 basis points	$0.50	$2.47	$4.88	$9.52	$13.93
75 basis points	$0.75	$3.68	$7.23	$13.93	$20.15
100 basis points	$1.00	$4.88	$9.52	$18.13	$25.92
150 basis points	$1.49	$7.23	$13.93	$25.92	$36.24
200 basis points	$1.98	$9.52	$18.13	$32.97	$45.12
250 basis points	$2.47	$11.75	$22.12	$39.35	$52.76

Note: Assumes continuous compounding

that charges 150 basis points for the next 20 years is roughly equivalent to investing $74.08 ($100 – $25.92) in a product that has the same gross return but charges no annual expense for the next 20 years.

Stated another way, if you invest $100 in a product that charges a 150-basis-point expense ratio per annum, you will, after 20 years, have the same amount of money as a person who invests only $74.08 in a product that has the same gross return but charges no expense ratio. This is *regardless* of the size of the investment's gross return over the two decades. In other words, the table does not depend on the assumed investment return. Do the math to convince yourself that the future doesn't matter. Regardless of how well or poorly the mutual funds perform, in exactly 20 years Mr. Smith (who invests $100 in the 150-basis-point fund) will have the same amount as Ms. Jones (who invests $74.08 in the zero-basis-point fund), as long as both funds earn identical gross returns. (As a technical aside, in this example we are compounding returns on a continuous basis.)

Let's examine another, more practical way of interpreting the table. Suppose you are currently investing in a product with an expense ratio of 200 basis points. Further, you are planning to hold this investment for the next 10 years. Now, let's assume you locate an investment with similar investment objectives but an expense ratio of only 100 basis points. The savings from switching to this product would be 100 basis points per year, which according to the table translates into $8.61 per $100 invested ($18.13 – $9.52), in today's dollars. Thus, if it cost you *less than* $8.61 in loads, fees, commissions, and sales charges to switch to the less expensive fund, it would probably be worth it. Otherwise, you might as well stay in the product that charges the 200 basis points.

So without passing judgment on fair expense ratios, the table should give you an indication of how a small drip every year can erode quite a big hole in your portfolio as time goes by.

Remember, if you invest $10,000 in a product with an expense ratio of 50 basis points, the money managers will extract roughly $50 each and every year, as long as you hold the investment. Drip, drip, drip . . . In fact, if your investments grow, which after all is the basic idea, then the company will take out even more than $50 every year. They will remove 50 basis points — half a percent of *whatever* you have invested. Of course, they do it behind the scenes on a daily or monthly basis, which makes the actual drip look really small. But like the dollar or two you could save by not buying coffee every morning, the amount soon adds up.

So in the context of variable annuities, the question is: Are the extra 74 basis points that you have to pay on a variable annuity — or $14 for every $100 invested over 20 years — worth the extra mortality benefit that they provide? (The tax benefit should not cost you anything, since the company doesn't take any risk or incur costs in order to provide it to you.)

The answer comes from a Monte Carlo computer simulation and probability analysis. I built a computer program that determines how much money would have to be withdrawn — under the guise of annual fees — to pay for the possible death benefit. This program creates thousands of hypothetical investment scenarios in which future investment returns are generated and people are "killed" in a random fashion according a pre-specified mortality table. In the event that one of the hypothetical investors dies while his or her account is showing a (relative) loss, the imaginary insurance company has to pay out, using the funds it accumulated while charging the annual insurance fee. In fact, this simulation methodology is exactly what any prudent insurance company should do prior to determining a proper charge for the death benefit.

In short, the computer simulation figures out, by repeated trial and error, how much money the insurance company has to set aside each and every year to cover the possibility that some people might die with their account showing a loss. This number should reflect the smallest annual fee that will still cover the guaranteed minimum death benefit.

To get a sense of the results, take a look at Table 4.2, which estimates the value of a simple return-of-premium guaranteed minimum death benefit.

Here is how to read this table. Let's take a 50-year-old

Table 4.2*

What is the value of the guaranteed minimum death benefit for a simple return-of-premium guarantee?

Age	Female	Male
30	0.3 basis points	0.4 basis points
40	0.8 bp	1.3 bp
50	2.0 bp	3.5 bp
60	5.0 bp	8.7 bp
65	7.6 bp	13.0 bp

**Assumptions:* *20% volatility, 6% risk-free rate, termination at age 75. 1994 GAM Table. See Notes section for further details on methodology.*

female who purchases a variable annuity that promises to return to her estate the original premium, if it's greater than the market value of the account when she dies. My computer simulations indicate that she should pay no more than 2 basis points of assets, per year, for this guarantee. Stated differently, the total value of the 2-basis-point fees that she will pay during the life of the product will exactly equal the total value of the insurance death benefit; and in most cases, the benefit won't be exercised at all. For men, the numbers are slightly higher, because the probability of death is higher. A 50-year-old man should pay 3.5 basis points for the guarantee.

Table 4.3*

What is the value of the guaranteed minimum death benefit on a single-premium variable annuity with a 5% roll-up?

Age	Female	Male
30	1.7 basis points	3.2 basis points
40	4.4 bp	7.9 bp
50	10.8 bp	19.2 bp
60	21.5 bp	37.5 bp
65	22.5 bp	39.3 bp

****Assumptions:** 20% volatility, 6% risk-free rate, termination at age 75. 1994 GAM Table, 200% cap. See Notes section for further details.*

Table 4.3 examines the "enhanced" guarantees. Specifically, it displays the fair mortality risk charge for a variable annuity that promises to return the original premium plus, at least, a 5% compounded interest rate at death. This is a more lucrative benefit than a simple return of premium, and the numbers reflect that. For example, a 50-year-old female that purchases this type of (enhanced) variable annuity should be charged 10.8 basis points for the guarantee. A male should be charged 19.2 basis points, due to the higher probability of death.

So, there you have it. I claim that the typical 50-year-old annuity buyer should be paying less than 5 basis points (2.0 bp for a woman and 3.5 bp for a man) for a return-of-premium guarantee. At this rate, the small but continuous fees that are charged on an annual basis add up over time, and fully pay for the potential death benefit. If the guaranteed minimum death benefit increases at 5% per annum (which is somewhat rare and lucrative), the fair insurance risk charge should be in the 10- to 20-basis-point neighborhood.

Now, these numbers represent pure costs, and the insurance companies, and sales force, are entitled to make a profit. But as you can see, with few exceptions, none of the numbers is anywhere near the extra 74 basis points that variable annuities charge for the death benefit. And when you look more closely at how the insurance companies come up with their fees, the value of the death benefit becomes even more suspect.

For example, it is interesting to note that the extra fees are not assessed according to age or sex. They are imposed as a strict percentage of assets, regardless of how old or young the contract owner is. This approach is in sharp contrast to life insurance, where your premiums depend almost entirely on your age and sex.

From a probability perspective, the unisex, age-independent nature of the death benefit expenses is quite puzzling. The risk of death is much higher for older males, compared with that of younger females, yet annual premiums — as a percentage of assets — are the same. If the extra fees are indeed meant to cover the "mortality risk" of dying during a bear market, then why are the fees not *based* on mortality risk?

Furthermore, you would expect that the value of the guaranteed minimum death benefit should correlate to the volatility of the underlying assets. In other words, the more volatile the asset returns, the higher the asset charge should be. In plain English, higher volatility simply means that the zigs and the zags are more pronounced. High-tech stock prices are more volatile than utility stock prices, which in turn are more volatile than boring old treasury bills.

If you want to buy insurance on your stock portfolio (for example, by using the type of put options I mentioned in Chapter 3), the price you pay will depend on the volatility and risk attached to the individual share prices. The more ups and downs, the more you should — and will — pay for the insurance. After all, you won't have to pay much for flood insurance if you live in Phoenix, Arizona. It's the chance of things going wrong that normally determines the premium.

But, lo and behold, the extra fees you pay for your variable annuity bear no relation whatsoever to the volatility of the assets in the variable annuity. Anyone who has ever purchased car insurance knows full well that it is more expensive to insure your 17-year-old son — who just got his driver's license — than it is to insure your 40-year-old spouse, who has been driving for 25 years. Why is that? Well, again, it's because the higher the chances of something going wrong, the more you have to pay to insure against it happening. The same pricing policy *should* apply to variable annuities, but it never happens. Why pay insurance fees on money market funds when the chances of losing money on them are basically zero? The people who determine VA risk fees don't seem to take this into account.

CONCLUSION

Variable annuities and mutual funds exhibit more similarities than differences. They both are savings vehicles that contain pools of managed money that are broadly diversified and should grow your money over time. However, when you purchase a variable annuity, you are paying an average of 74 basis points more in annual expenses than you would pay on an investment in a regular mutual fund. So what do variable annuity investors get in return for those 74 basis points? They get three things:

1. a guaranteed minimum death benefit
2. a guaranteed annuitization rate
3. tax-sheltered investment gains

Are these features worth the extra charge?

Well, one of the things I have tried to demonstrate in this chapter, by reporting the results of my Monte Carlo simulations, is that to an average 50-year-old, the standard guaranteed minimum death benefit is worth no more than 5 basis points. And the guaranteed annuitization rate is unlikely to be used by most people and is far too conservative (read: low) to be of much value. In fact, according to a recent survey sponsored by the Society of Actuaries, less than 1%–5% of variable annuity accounts are ever annuitized. So the only insurance benefit you are *really* getting is the death benefit. If the thought of dying during a bear market frightens you (or your children), you are probably better off buying a simple no-frills term life insurance policy that will pay its full face value upon your death regardless of whether the stock market is up or down. It will be much cheaper and will have more favorable tax consequences.

Of course, while you're still alive the tax shelter can be worth something to you personally, depending on your circumstances (such as when you have maxed out your 401(k), IRA, 403(b), and other qualified plans). But here is an important point to note when comparing equity mutual funds to equity-based variable annuities. Low-fee index funds that are managed in a tax-efficient manner would probably serve just as well. These tax-efficient funds strive to minimize the annual turnover (read: realized gains) and essentially create their own tax-deferred investment product — but with much lower fees!

So why are the VA fees so high? Where are the fees going, if not to cover the insurance risk? Well, for the most part, the extra basis points they are "siphoning" from your account are going directly to the broker or agent who sold you the variable annuity. Indeed, the commissions can be as high as 8% of the original investment in the variable annuity.

But on a deeper level, in my view, the most likely reason for the higher fees is that insurance companies have been granted monopoly power to manufacture a tax-favored product. Naturally, like all good monopolists (or even a cartel), they charge a price that far exceeds the product's cost of production.

Paying extra fees and expenses for the privilege of using tax breaks and shelters is not very different from the fact that yields on tax-free municipal bonds are always lower than yields on bonds of equal financial risk. Remember, the coupons on most municipal bonds are exempt from income taxation. And therefore, the yield on these bonds is lower because the after-tax return is higher. In a well-functioning financial market, the prices of these bonds are bid up, so that their *after-tax returns* are comparable to the after-tax returns from similar (non-tax-exempt) bonds.

If you are in a very low tax bracket, tax-free municipal bonds make little sense; you can do better with regular bonds. But if you're in a high enough tax bracket, then tax-free muni-bonds might be the right investment for you.

I believe the same thing can be said of the variable annuity market. The probabilities and computer simulations indicate that the value of the death benefit is much lower than the extra fees charged in the name of this guarantee. So, in my opinion, a very large portion of the extra charge implicitly goes toward paying for the privilege of tax deferral. You'll have to assess the value of that privilege carefully for your personal tax situation.

One last word of advice. If you do want to buy a variable annuity, don't put it in a qualified (tax-deferred) retirement plan. You'd be far better off reserving that space for investments that actually need the shelter. Otherwise, you are in effect taking two (expensive) umbrellas to work.

CHAPTER 5

Diversification:

What's Wrong with One Basket?

The famous economist John Maynard Keynes was once quoted as saying that he did not believe in diversifying his investments — he felt that you should simply buy a few good stocks and hold on to them. In stark contrast, Peter Lynch, the legendary Fidelity Investments guru, is rumored to have owned at one point more than 1,000 different stocks in his mutual fund portfolio.

Keynes's comments aside (how do you find those few good stocks, anyway?), it's pretty much accepted wisdom that diversifying your investments makes good strategic business sense. "Don't put all your eggs in one basket" was a philosophy preached long before the emergence of modern portfolio theory. In fact, the Babylonian Talmud, compiled more than 2,000 years ago, recommends that a person split his or her wealth into three parts. One-third should be placed in real estate, one-third in money, and the remaining third in business assets, which I liberally interpret to include equities. Overall, not bad investment advice, especially if you could have followed it for the last 2,000 years.

But in all seriousness, why does diversification work? After all, wouldn't you think that the more stocks you own, the more likely you are to catch a loser? Or at least that you're as likely to catch a loser as you are to bag a winner? Is it possible to be over-diversified and own too many stocks? And if it is possible, wouldn't these same general issues apply to mutual funds as well? There are now thousands of mutual funds available in the United States. Does any one mutual fund hold enough stocks to be labeled "diversified"? How many mutual funds should you own to be properly diversified? And finally, given the emerging global economy, how much international exposure should your investments have?

To answer these and related questions on the benefits of diversification, I'd like to present a slightly different perspective. More specifically, I want to focus on the core reasons for diversifying. And I want to do that, as you might have guessed by now, by examining the odds.

Before I get started, however, there's one thing that I should make clear about the whole subject of diversification. There is nothing inherently magical about splitting your money into many small parts and putting each part into a different investment vehicle. The benefit does not derive from the process of splitting the money, or placing it into different mutual funds.

Rather, it's the simultaneous movement of these investments that's important. In other words, how do they behave, move, and grow over time? Do they move in lockstep? If one zigs, does the other zag? Obviously, this is a critically important question, because if the various investments all move in the same direction at the same time, up or down, you're not likely to benefit very much from diversifying. If they're all moving up, you might as well pick one good fund, or stock for that matter, and stick with it. And if they're all moving down, then again, diversification clearly hasn't helped.

The key — and the secret — to successful diversification is an old axiom: opposites attract.

In investment terms, that means you want to diversify into sectors of the global and local economy that do not share the same up and down influences. For example, if you invest in both the financial services sector and the consumer products sector, you hope that when one is faltering, the other is not. Or if you further diversify into oil and gas and other resource industries, then ideally, if the first two sectors suffer, the third will prosper. The way to quantify, or measure, this parallel movement, is by using something statisticians label a correlation coefficient. This coefficient can range from negative 100% up to positive 100%. The language can be a bit technical, but the concept is simple, so let me explain how the correlation coefficient works, and why it is so fundamental to the investment process and diversification issues.

To make these concepts a bit more concrete, here's an example. Consider the following three stocks: Microsoft Corp., American Greetings Corp., and Gold Standard Inc. Figure 5.1 graphs the value of an initial $1,000 investment in each of the three stocks, charted between January 1995 and December 1998.

The initial $1,000 investment in Microsoft in January 1995 is worth $9,075 in December 1998. Similar initial $1,000 investments in American Greetings and Gold Standard in January 1995 are worth $1,652 and $21 respectively on December 1998. Clearly, Gold Standard was a huge disaster,

Figure 5.1 A Tale of Three Stocks

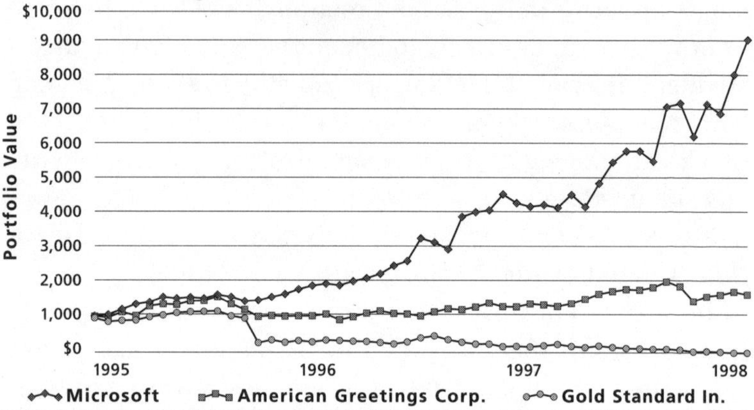

while Microsoft has made investment history. I hope you owned shares of the latter and not the former. (I also hope the U.S. justice system does not turn Microsoft into a Gold Standard.)

Now, assume you didn't have a crystal ball and that you decided to invest $1,000 in a portfolio consisting of equal weights of these three stocks; in other words, you diversified your portfolio by investing $333.33 in each. The $1,000 you invested in January 1995 is worth $3,582.91 in December 1998. As you can readily see, this diversified return is much lower than what you would have earned if you had invested in Microsoft alone. But it is also much higher than either the American Greetings or Gold Standard individual returns.

This example should give you an excellent indication of the pros and cons of diversification. On the one hand, diversification allows you to avoid disasters such as the Gold Standard returns. On the other hand, it prevents full realization of the returns on hyper-performing stocks, such as Microsoft.

So regardless of whether you are looking at three or 300 stocks, there's an implicit trade-off when you diversify. Still, there is universal agreement that diversification is an essential investment strategy. To understand why the benefits of diversification outweigh the potential gains of investing in a single outstanding stock, we have to consider the risk dimension. More specifically, we must recognize that the risk associated with a stock is really a combination of two types of very distinct risks. One is called *general market risk*; the other is called *individual security risk*. Let me briefly explain what I mean by these types of risk, and why it's important to keep track of both. After all, you might be saying to yourself, "I either make money or lose money."

General market risk refers to risk associated with stock-price changes that have nothing to do with an individual company, but are instead due to changes in the overall economy. General market risk is often referred to as *systematic risk*. For example, if the Federal Reserve decides to raise interest rates, it will affect the market as a whole, probably in a negative manner. In that event, there will be more stock sellers than buyers and share prices will fall. Similarly, if the economy were to slip into a recession, it would affect the entire market, not just a handful of stocks.

A stock whose price changes closely follow the price changes of the market, as proxied by a stock index, contains more general market risk than a stock whose changes are not closely related to changes in the general stock market. So general market risk is a useful measure of the relationship between the firm and the market. However, the firm also faces risks unrelated to market behavior. Individual security risk refers to the risk of stock-price changes that arise from events associated with the firm itself, independent of changes in the overall economy or the market. Individual security risk is often referred to as *unsystematic* or *unique risk*.

There are numerous potential sources of individual security risk. Sales may decline or rise sharply. The firm may fall victim to a fire, bad weather, lawsuit, or fraud. Alternatively, the company may acquire rights to a proprietary patent or may have abnormally excellent or incompetent management. All of the above, as well as their less dramatic parallels in day-to-day operations, may yield stock-price changes entirely independent of the broader market.

Obviously, there's an essential difference between market risk and individual security risk. Market risk cannot be erased by diversification; unique risk can. That's because the source of market risk is changes in the overall economy. This type of risk cannot be diversified away. On the other hand, security risk is firm specific. This type of risk can easily be diversified away. While a single firm may face a catastrophe on a single day, it is far less likely that a number of firms will face similar catastrophes on the same day. Hence, the importance of unique risk diminishes as the number of firms, or stocks, in the portfolio increases, as shown in Figure 5.2.

Figure 5.2 Total Risk vs. Number of Stocks

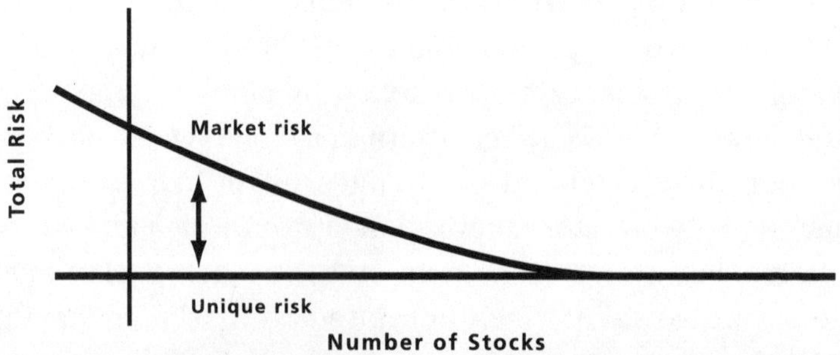

A fundamental axiom (or some would say religious belief) of modern economic theory is that investors are only rewarded for risks that cannot be diversified away. Individual security risk can be virtually eliminated by holding other stocks in the same industry or sector; general market risk cannot be eliminated by holding more of any industry or sector.

Here's an analogy. One of the more dangerous competitions athletes can participate in is auto racing. Unfortunately, we often read of fatal or life-threatening accidents during races. Clearly, an individual with an opportunity to participate in such a race will evaluate whether the danger associated with racing is offset by the many benefits, such as potentially high salaries, fame, the thrill of speed, and the sense of personal accomplishment. One can therefore perceive the expected value of these benefits as the reward for taking on the risk associated with participating in the races.

Now, let's suppose that you have agreed to drive in such a race but, for whatever reason, have also decided to forgo all of the protective gear typically used by race car drivers, such as protective helmets and clothing manufactured from inflammable materials. Clearly, you would be increasing your personal risk greatly. Is it sensible to argue that you should receive extra salary because of these additional risks?

The logical answer is no. Drivers cannot avoid certain risks associated with auto racing. Hence, these risks should be compensated. But if a risk can be avoided, why should you be compensated for acting carelessly? Since the proper protection can eliminate or reduce avoidable risk, there is no benefit to assuming such risk.

Now, to avoid complicating our discussion, we have focused so far on stock diversification. In reality, of course, an investor may choose to diversify not only across individual stocks or sectors, but across different types of investments and geographical regions.

Indeed, to appreciate the benefit of choosing an expanded diversification program, we should note that even the market portfolio has some risks that *can* be diversified away. In other words, there are unique risks associated with individual markets. Most investors trade in stocks of domestic firms in a particular market. Therefore, if that market were to experience a political or economic catastrophe, the domestic firms traded on the market would all be affected. But these events may have less of an effect on companies and stocks in other countries.

Through international diversification, an investor can avoid the risks associated with a single country. Note, however, that domestic events in some countries may affect international stocks as well. For example, it is difficult to insulate against unique risk associated with powerful economies like the United States or Japan, due to the impact that events in these countries have on other countries in their region or in the world.

Similarly, other types of diversification may be useful as well. Diversifying across different types of investments, such as fixed-income investments and real estate, can help reduce inflation risk. The value of fixed-income investments decreases as inflation increases. Conversely, the value of real estate increases as inflation increases. A portfolio containing both of these types of investments will be insulated against inflation risk.

Diversifying across investments with different levels of liquidity might be useful as well. Liquidity refers to the speed and cost with which investors are able to liquidate all or some of their portfolio, such as when faced with a medical emergency or a family business on the verge of bankruptcy. For example, real estate is commonly perceived as an illiquid investment, due to the time and various fees (agent, lawyer, taxes) associated with a purchase or sale. Conversely, money market investments can be quickly and cheaply liquidated.

Consider, for example, two national stock markets — the United States and Europe. If you think about it for a moment, you'll see that there are three broad possibilities for how these two markets might behave vis-à-vis one another or move over time. There's a positive correlation, a negative correlation, and no correlation.

The first possibility, the positive correlation, simply means that both markets move together in roughly the same average direction. When European stock markets are having a relatively strong week, month, or year, then U.S. markets are doing the same. And when European markets are experiencing difficult times, so are the U.S. markets. Again, this behavior is said to be positively correlated because both markets move in the same general direction at the same general time. They share the same ups and the same downs. The stronger (or closer) this parallel is, the higher the correlation coefficient. In fact, if the two markets moved in perfect lockstep, a statistician would say that they have a correlation coefficient of 100%.

On the other side, we have a negative correlation. This would mean, for example, that when one market does better than average, the other performs worse than average. When one market has a relatively good week, month, or year, the other has a relatively bad week, month, or year. In the extreme, a correlation coefficient of –100% implies that the markets move in exactly opposite relative directions.

Of course, in the new global economy, it's tough to find such negatively correlated markets. Indeed, more typically, a rising tide lifts all ships (and vice versa). But if you look hard enough, you should be able to find some market segments that are counter-cyclical to others.

Now, just to get a clearer sense of how this correlation thing operates, here are some numbers. For example, over the last 20 years, the correlation between U.S. equity returns and European equity returns has been roughly 60%. This — among other things — means that when the European stock market is having a better-than-average month, the U.S. market is also having a better-than-average month.

Reviewing the last two decades, statisticians have measured the strength of this positive parallel movement on a scale of 1 to 100 and come up with the number 60. This is definitely a positive correlation coefficient, but not necessarily a very strong correlation. Still, it makes a certain amount of intuitive sense that global capital markets should move at least partially in tandem.

So why am I so preoccupied with co-movements and correlations? Who cares if or how different markets move together? Well, as I suggested earlier, correlation is the key and secret to diversification's success.

Think of it this way. Suppose you are faced with two decent investment opportunities. You expect both to make you a few dollars. Moreover, there is a significant additional benefit: the two markets in which you might invest are not perfectly correlated. They do not move together in a parallel direction. Thus, you have a better chance to gain by holding both of them. Let me explain why. Assume that you split your money equally between the two investments. For various hypothetical correlation scenarios, Table 5.1 shows the probability that you will earn less than you would if you invested instead in a one-year term deposit earning 5%.

As you can see, in the most extreme case, when the correlation between the two investments is a perfect 100%, the probability of earning less than the term deposit is roughly 37% — very high, indeed. If you knew beforehand that there was almost a two-in-five chance that your investment would fare no better than what you could get from a very secure certificate of deposit at your neighborhood bank, you'd think twice, wouldn't you?

So it seems that with a perfect 100% correlation, there are absolutely no benefits to diversification. If you split your money into two baskets — baskets that are in exactly the same place (two markets that are perfectly correlated)

Table 5.1*

What are the odds of earning* less than *a one-year 5% term deposit if you split your money equally across two investments with certain correlation coefficients?

Correlation Between Investments	Probability of Shortfall
100%	36.94%
75%	35.33%
50%	33.43%
25%	31.11%
0%	28.18%
–25%	24.28%
–50%	18.63%
–75%	9.44%
–100%	0.00%

**Note: Both investments are expected to grow at an annual rate of 15%, with a standard deviation or volatility range of 30%. The probability that each individual asset will earn less than 5% is exactly 36.94%.*

— you have basically kept your eggs in the same basket. By analogy, then, if you diversify into a perfectly correlated investment, the odds of earning less than a standard 5% deposit are the same as if you did not diversify — and simply kept all your money in the one original investment.

At the other extreme is the correlation coefficient of –100%. In this case, if you split your money between two investments, the odds of earning less than a term deposit are reduced to a perfect zero. In other words, you will never do worse than 5%. You have basically taken two risky investments, put them together in your investment portfolio, and created a situation in which you will never lose money. Not bad at all. Wait a minute, you might be saying. What's the catch? How can I guarantee that you won't lose money?

Well, of course I can't. Remember, this is purely a hypothetical example in which the correlation coefficient is artificially set to –100%. In the real world, you can never really find such a situation. Think again about the example. If one investment does better than average by x%, when the other performs worse than average by x%, then the good return more or less nullifies the bad return, and you are left with the average. In sum, the perfect negative correlation means that any bad surprises from one investment will be offset by good surprises from the other asset. Put them both together in the same portfolio, and you have no surprises.

Now, you may be thinking that if the two investments are correlated in a negative fashion, why don't they completely cancel each other out, leaving you nothing at the end of the year? If one completely zigs when the other completely zags, shouldn't you be left with a flat profile?

Not exactly. Remember that negative (or positive) correlations are rarely 100%. More importantly, I did not say that when one investment goes up 8%, the other goes down 8%. I said that when one goes up by more than *the average* performance of the market, the other goes down by more than *the average* performance of the market.

Both investments, however, are expected to increase — in Table 5.1, I assumed an increase of 15% per year. The perfect negative correlation therefore means that when one market goes up 23% (8% more than the expected 15% average), the other will increase by only 7% (8% less than the expected 15% average). In other words, one has climbed 8% more than average, while the other has risen 8% less than average. But both have gone up.

Enough with perfect correlations. Let's take a look at the more reasonable and more common middle ground. In other words, let's see what happens when you diversify into investments that have correlations that are much greater than –100% and much smaller than +100%.

For example, in Table 5.1, you will see that if the correlation coefficient is exactly zero — i.e., there is absolutely no relationship between the two investments' movements — the probability of earning less than a 5% term deposit is roughly 28%. Compare that with the 37% chance of doing worse than the term deposit by having all your eggs in the same or one basket. This is a reduction of 37% – 28% = 9%.

In short, by splitting your money into two parts, you are reducing considerably the risk of underperforming the term deposit. Thus, as you can see, even though the correlation between the two investments is zero — i.e., if one does better than average, there is no indication of how the other will perform — there are still benefits to diversifying.

Similarly, if the correlation coefficient is –25%, the odds of your portfolio doing worse than the term deposit is 24% (or about one in four). Compare that with the 28% chance of doing worse when the correlation is zero. Once again, the benefits are clear. The lower the correlation between the two investments, the lower your risk.

I like to call this the fundamental law of diversification: "The risk of the sum is less than the sum of the risk."

What do I mean? Remember that you need two ingredients or factors for successful diversification. The first is non-perfect correlation; the second is an expectation of some profit from both investments. How much you benefit from diversification will depend on the strength of these two factors.

By investing in two imperfectly correlated assets, you are reducing the shortfall risk compared to the individual shortfall risks of each asset. Thus, the risk of the sum — or the risk of the portfolio that consists of two assets — is less than the sum of the risks — or just adding the risk of each individual asset.

Let me clarify this point by walking through a detailed example. We know that if you put $100 in a term deposit that pays 5% per annum, you'll have $105 at the end of the year. Not much of a payback, but very safe, very conservative. Now, let's pretend that you want to invest in the market, take some risk, and diversify. Instead of putting your money in the bank, you put $50 in one asset (let's call it Fund XYZ) and $50 in another (Fund ABC).

Now, we know from Table 5.1 that if there is zero correlation between the price movements of these two investments, then you stand a 28% chance of having less than $105 at the end of the year. This is what I call the risk of the sum. It's the risk of your capital, or the risk of your portfolio.

On the other hand, if you put the entire $100 in any one asset, either Fund XYZ or Fund ABC, the chance of earning less than $105 now rises to 37%. This is what I call the sum of the risk. The fundamental law of diversification in action means that the risk of the sum (28%) is less than the sum of the risk (37%).

An additional point to mention is that in Table 5.1, we are dealing with a one-year horizon. It examines the shortfall odds over a 12-month period. What happens if we extend this correlation analysis to a longer time horizon?

Table 5.2 paints the longer-term picture. This time, the returns on money split equally between two investments (in various correlation scenarios) are compared at five years (with a five-year 5% compounded deposit) and at 10 years (with a hypothetical 10-year 5% deposit).

As you can see, Table 5.2 has uniformly lower shortfall probabilities than those in Table 5.1. What does that mean? It means that the odds of earning less than a five-year compounded 5% term deposit decrease the longer you hold the investment. This concept was introduced in the Introduction, when I discussed the effect of time horizons on shortfall risk. As I argued then, the longer you hold an investment, the lower the probability of regret.

But even more important than the time-horizon effect in

Table 5.2*

When you split your money equally across two investments, with different correlation coefficients, what are the odds of earning

(a) less than a *5-year* 5% compounded term deposit?
(b) less than a hypothetical *10-year* 5% compounded term deposit?

Correlation Between Investments	5-Year Probability of Shortfall	10-Year Probability of Shortfall
100%	22.80%	14.59%
75%	20.00%	11.70%
50%	16.92%	8.79%
25%	13.53%	5.96%
0%	9.83%	3.39%
–25%	5.94%	1.37%
–50%	2.31%	0.24%
–75%	0.17%	0.00%
–100%	0.00%	0.00%

**Note: Both investments are expected to grow at an annual rate of 15%, with a standard deviation or volatility range of 30%. The probability that each individual asset will earn less than 5% compounded for five years is exactly 22.80%; for 10 years it is 14.59%.*

Table 5.2 is the fact that the amount by which the shortfall risk is reduced depends on the correlation coefficient between the two assets that you are mixing in your portfolio. In other words, the lower the correlation, the lower the risk.

Compare, for example, the zero correlation case. In Table 5.1 — looking at risk over a one-year period — the probability of shortfall was roughly 28%. In the case of a five-year horizon with zero correlation between the assets, the probability of shortfall is reduced to roughly 10%. Over 10 years, the same zero correlation between the two investments leads to a shortfall risk of approximately 3%. Isn't it remarkable what four — or nine — more years of investing can do?

The reduction is even more pronounced if you look at a negative 50% correlation. Remember, a negative correlation means that when one asset is doing better than average, the other is doing worse than average. In other words, they are generally moving in the opposite relative direction. The –50% is midpoint on a scale of –100% to 0%, and measures the relative strength of this opposite movement. In Table 5.1, the one-year horizon case, the probability of shortfall is roughly 19%. In Table 5.2, the five-year horizon, the odds are reduced to a mere 2%. For 10 years, it is reduced to less than a quarter of a percentage point. Notice the effect of time — and the effect of correlation.

What, then, are the lessons?

Two things will reduce the shortfall risk of your portfolio: (1) the longer time horizon over which you hold the portfolio; and (2) the movement of the assets in your portfolio. The more independently they move, the more your risk is reduced.

I like to argue that there are two dimensions to investment diversification — time and space. (No, I have not been watching too many *Star Trek* episodes.) By time, I mean the length of time you hold the portfolio; the longer you hold it, the more diversified your portfolio becomes. If you consider the essence of diversification to be the reduction of shortfall risk — owing to the imperfect correlation — then holding the portfolio for longer periods of time will also reduce shortfall risk.

I believe that if you invest in U.S. equities during the year 2000 and during the year 2001, you are essentially holding two different investments. Sure, they are the same asset class — namely, U.S. equities. But the returns from these two investments are most likely uncorrelated; that is, the return in one year is independent of the return in the next. If U.S. equities do better than average during 2000, the odds are still only 50/50 that they'll do better than average during 2001. So I would argue that you diversify your investments by holding both — equities in 2000 and equities in 2001. You see, in my opinion, the word "diversification" is not just about diversity at any one point in time; it's actually about investing in products that do not move together, so that your shortfall risk (probability of regret) is reduced. Therefore, investing for long periods of time in one asset is qualitatively similar to investing in different assets over one period of time.

By space diversification, I mean that the more independent assets you have in your portfolio (independent in the sense of not moving in tandem with each other), the more diversified the portfolio becomes. I chose the word "space" to reflect this principle because when you diversify across geographic and economic boundaries, you are likely — though not necessarily guaranteed — to find investment assets that move independently.

I do hope you grasp the main point that emerges from this general approach; specifically, the positive effect of more time (a longer holding period) and more space (more investments that move independently of each other) on your portfolio. Now let me address some of the real-world issues.

Practically speaking, if your investment portfolio is holding only U.S., broad-based equity investments, you are subjecting yourself — in one year — to a 37% risk of not beating a 5% term deposit. This conclusion comes from Table 5.1's one-year, perfect-correlation case. In any one year, there's almost a 40% chance that you will earn less than 5%. But if you can find and invest in another asset class, which is expected to increase, but is not perfectly correlated with your first, U.S.-based equity investment, you will gain from the law of diversification. And the less correlated this asset class, mutual fund, or investment is with the U.S. market, the greater will be your gain.

The same diversification principle, of course, is applicable to more than just national stock markets. Bonds, real estate, precious metals, commodities, and even art do not move with perfect correlation to U.S. equity markets. The actual correlations vary over time (more on this topic a bit later), but there is room for most of these asset classes in a well-balanced portfolio because they will all help to reduce your shortfall risk — the risk of doing worse than the risk-free, 5% benchmark. Remember the two ingredients, though. They must have imperfect correlation and they must have a reasonable chance of making some money over time. (The price of Elvis memorabilia is not correlated with the general stock markets, but I'm not sure about the growth prospects.)

So what, then, is the right amount for you? Precisely how much should you invest in each of these asset classes? What allocation is the right one given your circumstances? How much should you invest in the U.S., the U.K., Germany, or even Japan?

Good questions. Unfortunately, as is often the case with investment decisions, the answers depend on your personal circumstances, needs, requirements, fears, and phobias — otherwise known as your attitude toward risk. I cannot pretend to have a cookie-cutter, formulaic answer that will fit all possible contingencies. In fact, I am very much averse to computer programs that offer black-box solutions to your investment needs. You must discuss these issues with your financial planner, investment adviser, broker, or tax accountant.

My objectives here are, in that sense, more modest. I want to explain the general framework, to show you the odds, and to argue the benefits of diversification. I hope I've given you the information you need to ask intelligent questions and appreciate the underlying issues.

CONCLUSION

In this chapter, I have provided a simple explanation of why diversification is such an important concept.

On the one hand, diversification permits us to avoid a single stock or asset class with catastrophically poor returns. On the other hand, diversification prevents full realization of the returns on hyper-performing stocks or economic sectors. I have also argued that total stock market risk can be perceived as a combination of two types of risk. *Unique risk* is associated with stock-price changes due to events associated with a particular company or corporation; this type of risk can be minimized by properly constructing a diversified portfolio, meaning one containing investments whose movements are negatively correlated with one another. By contrast, *market risk* is associated with stock-price changes due to changes in the overall economy. Portfolio diversification cannot reduce this kind of risk — as an investor, you just have to grin and bear it. But market risk is what you are compensated for in returns, precisely because you cannot "diversify it away."

Here's something else to consider. You can meet your diversification objectives whether you invest in individual stocks or in mutual funds (although most people choose mutual funds for the savings in time and money that come with the economies of scale enjoyed by mutual funds). Today, most mutual funds own more than 30 to 40 stocks. The general consensus among researchers is that an appropriately diversified portfolio should have between 25 and 40 stocks, so even a single mutual fund should be sufficient for diversification purposes, unless the fund's stocks are specifically concentrated in a single characteristic, such as geographic region. In that case, you might want to pick one or two more.

If you want to be more hands-on, and construct your

own portfolio using individual stocks, just be careful to choose stocks that are expected to move up in the long run, but not together. And remember, full diversification involves both "space" and "time": spread your investments over regions, sectors, and asset classes, and stay invested year after year.

CHAPTER

6

Investing on Margin:

The Good, the Bad, and the Ugly

To my grandfather, who lived through the calamitous events of 1929 and the ensuing depression, the only phrase more odious than "stock market" was the term "borrowing to invest." The mere mention of debt, whether for consumption or investment purposes, was sure to provoke a long sermon on lessons to be learned from financial economic history.

Yet, at first glance, the notion of using other people's (the banks') money to invest, also known as leverage, appears quite alluring. Indeed, I am amazed by the number of otherwise prudent individuals who have recently thrown caution to the wind and — looking brilliant in hindsight — leveraged themselves to phenomenal returns.

Indeed, despite the problems it may have caused in the

past — and with all due respect to my late grandfather — I think that careful, judicious leveraging is a sure way to grow wealth. Still, it clearly has three distinct faces — what I call the Good, the Bad, and the Ugly.

Leverage, in this context at least, simply means borrowing money to invest. The phenomenal stock market returns experienced in recent years have tempted many investors into precisely that risky proposition. Unfortunately, if you succumbed to this strategy, the third quarter of 1998 probably taught you a lesson or two about the uglier side of leverage.

The basic arithmetic of leverage is simple and compelling. Suppose you have $10,000 invested in a mutual fund and the mutual fund goes up by 15% in one year. That means you've made $1,500 on your original $10,000 investment. Now, that's nice, but it could be a lot nicer. If you could somehow borrow an additional $10,000 (the equivalent of 100% leverage) and invest $20,000 ($10,000 + $10,000) in the mutual fund, you will have made a lot more by year's end.

With a 15% return, the $20,000 would become $23,000. Of course, from that amount you'd have to subtract the original loan of $10,000, plus any interest that you might have paid — say, $500 (5% on $10,000). That would leave you with $12,500. Wow! You started with $10,000 and turned it into $12,500, a full $1,000 more than if you had not borrowed. That's the equivalent of a 25% return. In other words, you've leveraged the fund's 15% return into a 25% return. That's what I call the Good.

Given the potential power of leverage, it's no wonder that investors, in high times, have rushed out to remortgage their homes, cottages, boats, and children to invest the proceeds in the stock market. As long as (after-tax) interest payments were lower than your earnings, you'd end up ahead of the game. In fact, if you borrowed $20,000 for every $10,000 you owned — a leverage factor of 200% — you could have earned 35% on your original $10,000 (and so on and so forth). The only constraint might have been a financial institution that placed restrictions on leverage or margining ratios — or perhaps a financial planner with some common sense.

So what could be wrong with this strategy?

Well, the arithmetic works in reverse as well. Yes, if markets move up by 15% a year, everything is peachy keen. But if markets suddenly drop 25% in one year (or worse, in one quarter), then you not only lose 25% on your original investment of $10,000, you lose 25% on the borrowed money as well. When it comes time to pay back the loan, the problems start to pile up.

For example, if you had borrowed $10,000 — for total assets of $20,000 — a 25% loss would wipe out $5,000 of your capital, leaving you with $15,000 at the end of the year. To add insult to injury, you must pay back the $10,000 loan, plus the (assumed) 5% interest. At year's end, therefore, your equity — your assets minus your liabilities — has dwindled to a mere $4,500. Your original equity investment of $10,000 has lost 55% of its value, even though the market (fund, stock) only fell 25%. That's the Ugly side of leverage.

So, should you leverage? Is it a good idea? Will you make money? After all, in the long run, markets go up, don't they? Well, by now you should know that there are no simple answers to these questions; all we can do is look at the odds.

Consistent with the theme of this book, we now ask the questions: What are the odds that you will benefit from leverage? What are the odds that you will regret exercising it?

First, let's take a good look at the upside. Let's say you are faced with a stock, mutual fund, or investment that is expected to earn 15% on average, in the long run. However, because there are no free lunches in the world, you have to contend with some risk. I assume that the volatility risk of this particular investment is 30%, which is a number I have used elsewhere in this book. So, facing this kind of investment, what happens if you leverage yourself?

You must pay particular attention to two factors — the leverage ratio and the borrowing (margin account) interest rate. Both will affect your outcome and the odds. The leverage ratio is the amount that you borrow to invest, expressed as a percentage of your original equity or capital. For example, if you have $10,000 and borrow $10,000, your leverage ratio is 100%. If you borrow only $5,000, your leverage ratio is 50%. If you don't borrow at all, your leverage ratio is 0%.

Next, the interest rate. This is simply the after-tax rate of interest that you'll be paying on the borrowed capital. In the present climate, the rate can range anywhere from 3% to 10%, depending on many considerations. The most important of these are your credit worthiness and the odds of your going bankrupt. Clearly, you want to borrow at the lowest possible interest rate, so that you get to keep as much of your market gains as possible.

Once you put the two factors together — leverage ratio and interest costs — you can do some intelligent analysis of how the leverage will affect your investments. The numbers in the following three tables come from a Monte Carlo computer simulation such as those I discussed in the Introduction and in previous chapters. In this case, the computer generates millions of different scenarios that estimate the probabilities of earning various return levels, both with and without leverage. The tables report the probabilities from a variety of outcomes.

Here's how to read Table 6.1. We'll assume that you are paying 5% interest on your margin account. If you leverage at a rate of 100% — one borrowed dollar for every dollar of

Table 6.1

Leverage: The Good
What are the chances of doubling the market?

	Interest Cost		
	3%	5%	7%
Leverage Ratio			
0%	30.9%	30.9%	30.9%
25%	37.4%	36.9%	36.4%
50%	42.1%	41.2%	40.3%
100%	48.0%	46.7%	45.4%
250%	55.7%	53.8%	51.9%

Assumption: *The market earns 15% on average and the volatility of the market is 30%.*

original equity investment capital — then the odds of earning double the market rate (2 x 15% = 30%) on your investment are 46.7%. In other words, the chances of converting $10,000 into $13,000 are about 47%. That's slightly less than a one-in-two chance of doubling the market.

Compare that to the chances of earning the same 30% (2 x 15%) if you don't leverage at all. Then, as Table 6.1 illustrates, your zero-leverage chances are a mere 31%. This is less than one chance in three. Notice the huge increase in the probability of doing very well — if you leverage. Sound tempting? Many have been lured.

Of course, as you can see from Table 6.1, if you have to pay more than 5% on your margin (borrowing) account, the odds of doing better than doubling the market will go down a bit. That's simply because the market has to earn even more — which is even less likely — in order to pay back your higher-interest borrowing. Likewise, if your interest cost is lower than 5%, your odds are somewhat better, but not by much. The real improvement in odds comes from higher amounts of leverage.

Look at the 250% leverage ratio case. Now, for the same

doubling-the-market result, at a 5% margin, the numbers increase to 54%. This is a 54% chance (better than one in two) that you will earn more than a 30% return on your original investment. In fact, the higher your leverage ratio, the better your odds — up to a point. It's not surprising that so many have rushed to leverage their capital: the odds look so good.

Now, however, let's examine the Bad, the downside. What are the odds that you will lose money? What are the odds, with leverage, that you will end up with less than when you started?

Table 6.2 shows what happens when things go wrong. Although the odds of doubling the market are much greater for the leverage case, the odds of losing money are higher as well. For example, if you leverage yourself at 100% with a margin cost of 5%, the odds of losing money — the chances of having less than your original equity capital at year-end — are 34%.

Thus, if you start with $10,000 and borrow $10,000, at year-end, after paying back your loan with interest, the probability of having less than $10,000 is 34%.

Table 6.2

Leverage: The Bad
What are the chances of losing money?

	Interest Cost		
	3%	5%	7%
Leverage Ratio			
0%	30.9%	30.9%	30.9%
25%	31.6%	32.0%	32.5%
50%	32.0%	32.8%	33.6%
100%	32.6%	33.8%	35.1%
250%	33.4%	35.2%	36.9%

Assumption: *The market earns 15% on average and the volatility of the market is 30%.*

Wait a minute, you say. Thirty-four percent is not that much higher than the 31% chance of losing money if you don't use leverage at all. In other words, there's only a 3% greater chance that using leverage will court disaster. That doesn't sound so bad, does it?

Is that the sum total of your risk?

Well, not exactly. Here's the Ugly.

To give you an indication of how ugly things can get with leverage, Table 6.3 provides the probability of losing a quarter of your initial investment from a leveraged transaction. The question is: What are the odds that if you start off with $10,000 — and borrow — you'll be left with less than $7,500 after 12 months? This would be a 25% loss of equity capital.

If you don't leverage at all, the chances of suffering such a drastic reduction of capital are about 9%. But if you choose the 100% leverage route, and you pay a margin interest cost of 5%, your odds of losing a quarter of your initial investment are close to 20%. That's a one-in-five chance. Why are the odds so high? How can the odds of

Table 6.3

Leverage: The Ugly

What are the chances of losing a quarter of your initial investment?

	Interest Cost		
	3%	5%	7%
Leverage Ratio			
0%	9.1%	9.1%	9.1%
25%	12.6%	12.9%	13.1%
50%	15.3%	15.9%	16.4%
100%	19.3%	20.2%	21.2%
250%	25.2%	26.8%	28.4%

Assumption: *The market earns 15% on average and the volatility of the market is 30%.*

doing so poorly be so high? After all, the odds of doing very well were quite high as well. How can the odds be so high for both the Good and the Ugly?

Well, that's the key point with investment leverage. You are subjecting yourself to extremes. Things can go very well — or very badly. Very well if the market goes up; very badly if the market goes down. I like to say that leverage exaggerates both the severe upside and the severe downside.

On a technical level, you have increased the potential return of your investment, but you have increased the uncertainty as well. The higher uncertainty means that you are more likely to experience the extreme cases. In the good times, the extremes will be welcome. In the bad, they can bring you to the brink of bankruptcy.

Of course, it's unfortunate that you must take the bad (downside risk) with the good (upside potential). But that's precisely why most investment houses and regulators justifiably prohibit large amounts of leverage at the retail level (large companies seem to be exempt). There is, however, one way to eliminate — or at least greatly reduce — the chances of a wretched outcome. That is, buy a product with upside potential, but that can't lose money. Sound impossible? Well, investments with money-back guarantees, such as index-linked notes and put-protected portfolios, are all products that eliminate the possibility of events where your final wealth is *less* than your initial wealth.

These crash-proof investments, in all their guises, promise to return your original principal in the event of a bear market (or worse), although you'll pay for this feature with marginally lower returns. This essentially guarantees that if you've used leverage, you will have enough money to pay back your outstanding loan at maturity.

Of course, there is no guarantee that the return on these products will beat the interest costs that you must pay on your borrowings, but at least the chance of a true catastrophe is eliminated. In sum, the most important thing to remember when contemplating leverage is that you must be able to afford the interest payments, without having to sell out at the worst possible time.

CONCLUSION

In this chapter, we looked at whether using leverage — "borrowing to invest" in the purest sense — is a prudent strategy. First, if your interest cost is tax-deductible, and market returns are treated as capital gains — deferred as long as you don't sell — then the upside of leverage can look quite appealing. By the same token, the downside is obvious. If things go wrong — and they certainly can — your loss is magnified. As Table 6.3 demonstrated, the odds of suffering a severe loss of your original equity are quite high.

Once again, I have calculated and reported the odds. Now, you must decide whether to take the umbrella.

CHAPTER

7

Asset Allocation After Retirement:

How to Avoid Outliving Your Money

"Happy 65th birthday, Mr. Carlyle," sings the cheery voice at the other end of the telephone line. "It's now time to sell all your stocks and put the money in safe term deposits and savings bonds. After all, at your age, you can no longer afford to be taking those kinds of risks."

I certainly hope you never receive such a ridiculous phone call — especially not on your 65th birthday. But the underlying assumption, that retirees can't afford to take financial risks, seems to be widespread among the investing public.

And it's precisely that assumption that I want to explore in this chapter. More specifically, I want to examine the interaction between age, investment, and financial risk. Ideally, by examining the odds, I would like to answer the following question: What is an appropriate asset allocation for retirees?

The issue has two cogently argued sides. On the one hand, because of your age, you supposedly have a short investment horizon ahead of you, and therefore lack the time needed to recover from any losses you might incur from owning a portfolio heavily weighted in equities. On the other hand, if you shift your investment assets to fixed-income products — especially when interest rates are mired at historically low levels — your earnings will decline, perhaps to the point of jeopardizing your standard of living.

Therefore, before I begin any discussion of investment strategies for retirees, you must determine the extent to which you will be dependent on your financial assets to sustain your standard of living. Financial planners commonly refer to this as a "needs analysis."

What standard of living would you like to maintain during your retirement years? Do you want to travel the world? Will you stay at home? How expensive do you anticipate your lifestyle to be? These questions may not be as easy to answer as they seem. They certainly involve making important assumptions about your lifestyle preferences and market prices. But the bottom line is that you — and only you — can estimate how much you'll require on an annual basis to maintain your desired standard of living in retirement. Ideally, this "needs analysis" should be conducted many years prior to retirement — so that you can better save for your goals. But at the very latest, you should do it at age 65.

Of course, if you qualify for Social Security or a private pension, remember to subtract that amount from your annual needs. The objective is to get a desired number — an annual income level — that can be funded by your total financial assets. Without a good feel for what you'll need, it's meaningless to talk about appropriate investments to finance those needs.

Once this first stage is out of the way, once you know (in current dollars) how much you will need every year in retirement, we can move on to stage two. There we discuss an appropriate asset allocation for your retirement years. But please bear in mind that we may have to revisit stage one — most likely to lower the desired annual income level — once you see how much money you'll need to comfortably support your anticipated standard of living. For the moment, however, let's maintain a positive attitude.

Now, at the risk of being considered a complete simpleton, I'd like to start this analysis by stating the obvious. If, at age 65, you have liquid financial assets that are 100 times greater than your anticipated needs (the annual consumption requirements), then no matter how you invest during your retirement years, you will never run out of money. Of course, very few Americans are fortunate enough to be in this category. But presumably, those who are have no reason to change their investment philosophy at retirement.

Furthermore, at the risk of being considered coarse, if at age 65 you have liquid financial assets that are only five times greater than your desired annual income level, you are, quite frankly, doomed. If this is your situation, go back to stage one and re-budget. Or delay your retirement for a few more years. You certainly won't be able to invest your way out of this conundrum.

With these polar extremes out of the way, we are ready to address the question of an appropriate asset mix to support your desired annual consumption requirements. In other words, given your desired standard of living, what asset allocation — or mix between stocks, bonds, and short-term reserves, such as money market funds — will minimize the probability that you will run out of money during your retirement years? A little later in this chapter, I will flip the question around and ask the exact opposite: What is a sustainable real standard of living, given a particular wealth level?

So without further ado, let's look at some hypothetical numbers.

You've just retired at age 65 with fairly decent Social Security and company pensions, which should provide a large portion of your needs on an annual basis. In addition, after many years of contributing to a 401(k), IRA, or 403(b) plan, you've managed to build a nest egg of approximately $200,000, which is currently sitting in an assortment of mutual funds, term deposits, and other minor investments that you don't much care for. Your house, fortunately, is fully paid for, and you have no other major liabilities.

After conducting a needs analysis, taking full account of your lifestyle choices and retirement plans, you've determined that you require — in addition to your pension — approximately $10,000 each and every year until the end of your life. Naturally, you hope that your nest egg will be able to provide this additional amount.

Before we continue, I should clarify what I mean by $10,000 per year. This estimate assumes that today's prices — on which you based your needs — will remain the same throughout your retirement. In other words, it assumes that the inflation rate for goods and services will be zero for the next 30 years. Rather unrealistic, I'm sure you'd agree. True, inflation has averaged less than 3% almost every year since 1991. But there is no guarantee that the rate cannot or will not increase.

Economic history teaches us that price inflation can resurface suddenly and dramatically. Furthermore, the projected inflation rate for retirees may in fact be higher than the general inflation rate for the population at large. Think of the cost of geriatric medical care over the years.

Therefore, a better way to deal with long-term planning (given inflation uncertainty) is to budget and state your needs in real, after-inflation terms. At the same time, you must also project your investment returns in real, after-inflation terms. Let me explain.

As I said earlier, you essentially want to consume $10,000 "today" dollars for the rest of your life. By real consumption, I mean that you will consume $10,000 in your 65th year, $10,000 multiplied by the first year's inflation rate in your 66th year, $10,000 multiplied by the first and second years' inflation rates in your 67th year, and so on. However, to keep things in balance, when I talk about what your money can earn, I will look at returns in after-inflation terms as well, to account for the fact that your needs were expressed in the same framework.

Ideally, your pension plan comes with some form of inflation protection — or indexing — as well. (Ask your benefits administrator about it.) The indexing can be implicitly tied to the consumer price index (CPI) or to the performance of some investment fund.

Practically speaking, the easiest way to get at the $10,000 you'll need each year (about $833 per month) is to set up a systematic withdrawal plan that sells an appropriate number of stocks, mutual funds, or bonds each month to create the desired cash flow. This is like a reverse dollar-cost averaging strategy. Instead of buying an arbitrary number of units with a fixed amount of cash each month, you are selling an arbitrary number of units to create a fixed amount of revenue each month. Then, to account for any price inflation in your consumption needs, you increase the amount withdrawn under the systematic plan on a yearly basis.

Now, before we proceed, we must deal with one other unpleasant aspect of financial budgeting for retirement — income taxes.

The $10,000 that you need each year probably does not account for income taxes. So if you are planning to consume $10,000 from your nest egg each year, you will probably have to withdraw more than that, because of the income taxes that will be due. Everything you pull out of your tax-sheltered plan will be taxed at your marginal tax bracket because you've never actually paid income tax on that money (for the most part). Remember, those funds were deducted from income in the year that you made your contributions.

What this all boils down to is that if you need $10,000 to live on — and you're in a 33.33% marginal income tax bracket, for example — then you will really have to withdraw $15,000 from the nest egg. One-third of it will go to federal and state authorities (and back, very indirectly, to you, taking the optimistic and patriotic view); the other two-thirds you will be able to consume yourself. Yes, it sounds a bit depressing and drastic. But consider the bright side: you have never paid any income tax on that money, and it has grown, tax-deferred, for all those years. (Just to err on the conservative side, I'm not factoring in here certain expenses — for example, medical expenses — that may be tax deductible.)

Now, a Pandora's box that I would certainly like to avoid is the whole question of what your marginal tax bracket will be 10 or 20 years from now. Today, we know that the highest marginal tax bracket is in the 30% to 40% range. But who's to say that federal and state authorities won't raise that number, especially as it applies to funds withdrawn from a tax-sheltered savings plan? In fact, on a professional level, I feel much more confident predicting the long-term expected rate of return from various asset classes than I do predicting what the income tax structure will look like in 15 years. We might move toward a flatter tax system, in which all income is taxed at roughly the same rate; or we may see an increase in progressivity, which would raise tax rates on the wealthiest above the current 30% to 40% region. Unfortunately, I can't give you the odds on this one, and it's probably one of the biggest question marks in the financial planning equation. Nevertheless, we must play the game of life based on the current rules, and we must therefore make plans based on the current tax system.

Let me recap what we have done. By this point, you should have a pretty good sense of your needs, and those needs should be specified on a pre-tax basis. In the example we've been using, you have $200,000 in a tax-sheltered plan, and each year you will need to consume or withdraw $15,000, in after-inflation, pre-tax terms.

Roughly speaking, therefore, your Needs-to-Wealth (abbreviated as NtW) ratio is $15,000/$200,000 = 7.5%. Another way of looking at it is to say that your annual income needs represent 7.5% of the initial wealth available to support those needs. Thus, if you had $400,000 and your needs were $30,000, you would also have a 7.5% Needs-to-Wealth ratio. This ratio is important because it gives you a general sense of what kind of investment returns you'll require to support your annual needs. I would argue that all people — at age 65 — with a 7.5% NtW ratio are more or less in the same boat. That's because whether they have $1,000,000 or a mere $100,000 at retirement, they all have the same relative needs. (Of course, a millionaire's "needs" probably include luxuries that could be jettisoned if necessary.)

We are now ready to revisit the main question. Is $200,000 enough to support your $15,000 annual needs? The answer, of course, really depends on what you do with — or how you invest — the $200,000. Another way of asking the question is, can you sustain a NtW ratio of 7.5%? The answer to this question clearly depends on your asset allocation, on what your investment portfolio looks like during your retirement years.

First of all, let's see if you'll be able to live on interest and dividends alone. Evidently, the $200,000 will have to generate exactly 7.5% in order to create $15,000 — after inflation and before taxes. Unfortunately, money market instruments will earn you nowhere near that amount. So you have a clear choice: you can invest in these relatively safe investments, knowing that eventually you will have to encroach on your capital and may run out of money; or you can invest a bit more aggressively, and hopefully build your capital. (Or, of course, you can always decide to reduce consumption.)

The math is relatively simple. If your money earns a fixed 5% in real terms, and you consume $15,000 (in real terms) each and every year, you will run out of money in precisely 22 years. That's because the present value of $15,000, discounted at the rate of 5%, is exactly equal to $200,000. Stated differently, a $200,000 mortgage, amortized at a rate of 5%, will be paid off in exactly 22 years, when the annual payments add up to $15,000.

Okay, you say to yourself, if I can earn a consistent 5% every year (in real terms), my money will last for exactly 22 years. That's plenty of time, no?

Well, maybe, or maybe not. Statistics tell us that a man at age 65 has a 23% chance of living for 22 more years; a woman has a 40% chance of living for 22 more years (we'll discuss this in some detail in Chapter 8 when we look at mortality tables). So let's put two and two together and see what happens.

If you earn 5%, you'll run out of money in 22 years. That much is clear. But there's a 23% chance (40% for women) of living for more than 22 years. In other words, there is a 23% (40%) chance of outliving your money, if you earn 5% each and every year. Why? Well, the odds of outliving your money are the odds of being alive when the money runs out. If you know exactly when the money will run out, and you know the odds of living to that point, put them together and you have the odds of outliving your money.

Similarly, if your $200,000 nest egg earns a fixed 4% in real terms, you will run out of money even sooner — in exactly 19 years — because you are earning less. And the odds of living for 19 more years are, not surprisingly, higher than the odds of living for 22 more years. The chances are 33% for men and 52% for women. So if you earn 4% each and every year, the odds of running out of money are 33% and 52% respectively.

Another way of saying this is that slightly more than three of every 10 men (and one of every two women) will outlive $200,000 invested at 4%, if their annual pre-tax needs are $15,000.

Again, here's the procedure: Simply compute when the money will run out, then look at the probability of being alive at that time. The higher the number, the more likely it is that your standard of living is simply not sustainable. At some point, you will have to reduce your withdrawals, or recalculate your needs, to avoid starvation.

The same formula applies in the other direction. If your capital can earn 6% in real terms, you won't run out of money for 27 years. For a 65-year-old, 27 years may seem pretty far out in the future. Indeed, men at that age have only an 8% chance of living that much longer (and running out of money); women have a 20% chance. These figures are low, but not entirely comforting, especially for women.

Finally, if you are lucky or smart enough to have your capital earn 7.5% each year — you'll notice it works out to $15,000 each year — you will never run out of money.

Another way to think of this is that a $200,000 mortgage, amortized at 7.5%, with annual payments of $15,000, will never be paid off. You will barely manage to pay the interest, let alone pay down the principal.

So what are the odds of running out of money when

your capital earns 7.5% each and every year? Well, I hope you see that they are zero for both men and women. In fact, even if you earned slightly less (7.25% each year), you would run out of money in exactly 45 years. And the odds of being alive then are virtually zero for both genders.

No great secrets here, then: the less you earn, the sooner your money will run out, assuming that you'll need $15,000 in real terms each year.

Incidentally, all of these calculations can be easily performed with the aid of a calculator or spreadsheet, and then you can examine the odds from a mortality table. This calculation is essentially a mortgage amortization schedule that tells you when the money will run out, as opposed to when the mortgage will be paid off.

Table 7.1 puts a different spin on mortality statistics by looking at when your money will run out, and then stating the probability of living to that age.

What does this chart reveal? Well, for one thing, it tell us that if (at age 65) your financial plan is only valid for 20 years (age 85), there's a 47.9% chance for women (29.5% for men) that you'll still be alive when you run out of money.

Table 7.1

The Probability of Starvation (or, What is the probability of living to various ages?)

(Your current age is: 65)

To Age:	Male	Female
70	86.6%	92.7%
75	69.5%	81.9%
80	49.6%	66.8%
85	29.5%	47.9%
90	13.3%	27.8%
95	3.9%	11.4%

(Source: U.S. Decennial Life Tables for 1989–1991, Centers for Disease Control and Prevention)

This is the probability of outliving wealth. It is the probability of still being alive when there is no more money in the account.

Now, you're probably thinking that anyone in that situation would realize that they were about to run out of money and would lower their annual consumption. And in all likelihood, social support payments would kick in long before disaster struck. Or their children might be able to lend financial support. Nobody, in other words, really starves.

I agree wholeheartedly; nobody would actually reach starvation. Certainly, nobody would withdraw that final year's sum of $15,000 and then say, "Oops, what do I do next year?" But the idea is to plan ahead and to realize the consequences of your actions in their most drastic, worst-case forms. To avert a potential crisis, you must do one of two things, now: (a) invest more aggressively, so that you earn more return on your nest egg, or (b) cut down on your consumption — in other words, reduce your needs.

But here is the $200,000 question. What if you don't know exactly what your rate of return will be? Sure, with perfect foresight of investment returns, you would know precisely when the money would run out and you could then talk about the chances of living to that point. But in fact, nobody can know with utter certainty when his or her money will run out, because nobody can know with utter certainty what the annual rate of return will be. So how can we perform this exercise in the real world, where market returns fluctuate on a day-to-day basis?

Well, here is where the probabilities come in again. We are now ready for the full-fledged model. I call it the dual uncertainty model because there are really two sources of uncertainty that you have to concern yourself with, the investment probabilities and the mortality probabilities.

So we are going to work with two sources of randomness. The first is the probability of earning a particular rate of return. The second is the probability of living to a particular age. Of course, the odds of earning a specific return depend on your asset allocation — that is, on how you divide your capital between stocks, bonds, and other investments — and we will account for that explicitly. We will look at the odds, depending on how aggressively you decide to invest.

The technical question I want to investigate is: What asset allocation would maximize the probability that you will be able to consume $15,000 annually for the rest of your life?

Before I get into a full-throttle explanation, here is a sample table.

Table 7.2

What is the probability of outliving your money, depending on asset allocation?

(Current age is 65; initial wealth is $200,000; annual real withdrawal is $15,000; NtW Ratio is 7.5%)

Equity Allocation*	Male	Female
0%	38.1%	61.4%
20%	27.4%	46.0%
40%	19.8%	32.7%
60%	14.9%	23.7%
80%	12.1%	18.3%
100%	10.4%	15.6%

**The remaining wealth, that portion not allocated to the equity market, is invested in short-term deposits or money market funds.*

What does this table tell us? It tells us, for example, that if a 65-year-old woman allocates all of her $200,000 to short-term bank account or money market funds, and has zero exposure to the equity markets, there is a 61.4% chance that she will not be able to consume the desired $15,000. In other words, with a real consumption level of $15,000, there's a 61.4% chance that she will outlive her money. In contrast, a 65-year-old man who allocates 0% to equities will have a 38.1% chance of outliving his money. This number is still quite high, but as you probably guessed, it's lower than the woman's probability because men don't usually live — and consume — as long as women.

Now, what happens if you invest in — or allocate your assets to — funds with somewhat greater variability, but higher long-term growth rates? The fluctuations may hurt in the short term, but what do the overall odds look like when you take account of mortality and investment risk?

The answers are contained in the table. As the 65-year-old moves into a more aggressive allocation to equity, the probability of outliving wealth, surprisingly, decreases. For example, with a 60% allocation to equity, women have a 23.7% chance of running out of money; men have a 14.9% chance.

The higher average long-term rate of return counteracts the effects of the equity investment's short-term volatility, yielding lower "starvation odds."

Your question at this point, of course, is how and where did I come up with these numbers? Well, once again I used the method of Monte Carlo simulation, which I described in the Introduction. To remind you, I and some colleagues at York University constructed a computer program — a digital roulette wheel, if you will — that generates millions of different scenarios for the financial markets and human mortality. In one scenario you live to the ripe old age of 95; in another scenario you live to age 75. Some scenarios show the stock market booming for the next 20 years; others indicate a 10-year bear market. The probabilities — or relative occurrences — for these human life-span scenarios are taken from the Centers for Disease Control (U.S. Decennial) mortality tables; the probabilities for stock market and interest-rate evolution are generated using historical statistical estimates.

In one scenario, the computer predicted that the U.S. stock market would fall by 15% in one month. The computer certainly didn't give a reason. It didn't explain *why* that would happen. It simply said that it was within the realm of possibility. And lo and behold, during August of 1998, the S&P 500 index fell by roughly that amount. Quite uncanny!

Obviously, this doesn't mean that the computer actually predicted the future. It simply means that, using the Monte Carlo simulation, it computed a remote possibility of the market's declining by 15% in one month — and, implicitly, recommended that we should plan for such a possibility. I don't want to alarm you unnecessarily, but in a few scenarios it generated drops even scarier than 25%; fortunately, the computer estimated the odds of such events to be very small.

Now comes the fun part. After leaving the computer on all night, running millions of these future scenarios, we returned in the morning and started counting.

Specifically, for each and every possible asset allocation, we counted the number of times that the 65-year-old who consumes $15,000 per year will run out of money before he or she dies. These are the people who (theoretically) starve. The remaining people, who die with wealth, have managed to avoid outliving their money. The ratio of the former to the latter provides us with the probability of outliving your money. We then sift through the cases to locate the asset allocation that minimizes the probability of outliving wealth.

Let's look at an example. In one simulation, a 65-year-old woman who invested all of her capital in the stock market — consuming 15,000 real dollars each year — ran out of money in roughly five years because she had the uncanny bad luck of investing right before a horrendous (computer-generated) bear market. Again, however, the computer assigned a very low probability to this event.

In another scenario, we found that a 45-year-old man was able to take (very) early retirement, with only $200,000 in wealth, and still manage to consume $15,000 per year for life, by investing completely in equities. But this is because the computer killed him off at age 68, long before his full life expectancy. (I think it was a skydiving accident.) The computer also assigned this event — a robust stock market combined with early death — a very low probability. Overall, the chance that a man will be able to retire at age 45, with only $200,000 to support a spending habit of $15,000 per year, is not great.

Before I go further, I must emphasize the assumptions that go into such a Monte Carlo simulation study. First, as I mentioned, I assumed that future human longevity patterns would obey the above-mentioned U.S. Decennial life tables. If you believe that you are healthier than the average American — and that these numbers do not apply to you — then your probabilities of outliving your wealth are even higher than the above estimates. Remember, if you live longer, you consume longer; all else being equal, that increases the odds of starvation. Indeed, if you use a different mortality table, such as those for select population groups, the probability of survival can be much higher.

Second, I assumed that the real, after-inflation rate of return from short-term cash, or money market funds, would be 1.3% per annum. Yes, I know that the current rate on bank deposits is closer to 5%. But keep in mind that the inflation rate is about 3%, and we are concerned here with real — after-inflation — returns. So projecting ahead, a 1.3% return does not sound unreasonably conservative. Indeed, if you strongly believe that you can earn more than that — in real terms — without incurring any market volatility risk, then your probability of outliving wealth and running out of money will be lower. If you examine the real return from treasury bills over the last 50 years, the number is exactly 1.3%. So, although history is not the best of indicators for the future, I feel comfortable with this forecast.

Third, I assumed that the long-term real rate of return from the equity markets would be 9.3%, with a volatility of 15%. Both these numbers correspond with the behavior of American equity markets during the last 50 years. Please note: I am not assuming that you will earn 9.3% in real terms each year. Rather, I'm assuming that in the long term, you'll earn an average of 9.3% per annum, with a volatility of 15%. (Remember that volatility is a measure of how wide the spectrum of investment returns is expected to be. A volatility number of 15% means that 95% of the time, the returns will be within 2 x 15% = 30% of the expected value.) On the other hand, the nominal, pre-inflation, 25%–30% returns that North American markets have experienced in recent years cannot persist in the long run. In fact, even 9.3% may be a bit aggressive; a variety of financial commentators believe that the equity risk premium, as it is called, will be much less than observed in the past.

Finally, don't forget transaction costs. I very much doubt that you can earn a consistent, long-term 9.3% in real terms by investing in an equity fund with expenses of 1%–2%. Low fund expense ratios are crucial.

Now, obviously, the age (65) and the NtW ratio (7.5%) may not apply to your precise situation. So let's examine the odds for age 75, with the same NtW ratio of 7.5%. In this case, you are 75 years old, own a nest egg of $200,000, and want to withdraw $15,000 every year.

A few things should be immediately evident from Table 7.3. First, the probability of outliving wealth is uniformly lower at all asset allocation levels. For men, the "starvation probability" numbers range from 12% to 4%, much lower (and much better) than the 38% to 10% range we had for a 65-year-old in the same situation. The reason is quite simple: you are 10 years older and therefore have 10 fewer

Table 7.3

What is the probability of outliving your money, depending on asset allocation?

(Current age is 75; initial wealth is $200,000; annual real withdrawal is $15,000; NtW Ratio is 7.5%)

Equity Allocation*	Male	Female
0%	12.3%	22.1%
20%	9.1%	17.3%
40%	6.8%	14.3%
60%	5.5%	12.7%
80%	4.7%	12.1%
100%	4.3%	12.1%

**The remaining wealth, that portion not allocated to the equity market, is invested in short-term deposits or money market funds.*

years of consumption ahead of you. The odds of outliving your money, therefore, must be lower.

The same applies for the 75-year-old woman; her numbers now range from 22% to 12%. That's higher than it is for a man because women typically live longer. But these numbers are also lower than the same numbers for a comparable 65-year-old woman, which were 61% to 15%.

Another interesting thing to note about Table 7.3 is that the numbers level off at a 60% allocation to equity. In other words, any additional allocation doesn't do much to reduce the probability of shortfall or starvation. Why is this? Shouldn't higher levels of equity continue to reduce the starvation numbers? Well, the fact is that higher equity allocations will increase the growth rate of your portfolio in the long run. But in the short run, there's always some risk of a bad run of luck. Stated differently, with a 100% allocation to equities, there's a 4.3% to 12.1% chance that in the first few years you will experience negative returns, thus causing an erosion of capital from which you cannot recuperate in time.

Table 7.4

What is the probability of outliving your money, depending on asset allocation?

(Current age is 55; initial wealth is $200,000; annual real withdrawal is $15,000; NtW Ratio is 7.5%)

Equity Allocation*	Male	Female
0%	75.6%	93.2%
20%	59.4%	81.1%
40%	42.9%	61.4%
60%	30.8%	43.5%
80%	23.4%	31.8%
100%	19.3%	25.4%

**The remaining wealth, that portion not allocated to the equity market, is invested in short-term deposits or money market funds.*

To give you a sense of the richness of the Monte Carlo approach, here's another collection of simulated scenarios. This time, we looked at a 55-year-old, perhaps interested in early retirement.

From Table 7.4, we can see that a woman who consumes $15,000 every year from an original nest egg of $200,000 has a 93% chance of outliving her wealth, if all of the money is invested in short-term deposits or money market funds. Essentially, with that kind of a low-volatility (and low-return) asset allocation, there is no hope for an early retirement. At the other extreme, with a 100% allocation to equities, the odds of starvation are cut by three-quarters. As you can see, the probability of outliving wealth is reduced to 25.4% with a complete allocation to the equity market. Granted, a 25.4% chance of starvation is still rather intimidating, and not tolerable by any means. But the dramatic reduction from 93% to 25% is persuasive, and yields insight into the power of long-term equity growth, despite the associated volatility.

The male numbers are lower — remember, men don't

live as long and therefore consume less — but the odds are still quite high. The male starvation numbers range from 75% to 19%, not a very reliable way to retire. The message, however, remains the same: The best odds come from a higher allocation to the (volatile) risky asset class.

I would conclude that — especially for women — early retirement at age 55, with a 7.5% Needs-to-Wealth ratio, is unsustainable no matter how you allocate the funds.

But what if you take early retirement and consume less than $15,000 per year from your $200,000 nest egg? In other words, what if your Needs-to-Wealth ratio is lower? Intuitively, you would expect to be better off, in the sense that your odds should look better. What about if you retire at age 60 and invest in both stocks and bonds? What if you consume $20,000 for the first ten years in retirement, but $10,000 after that? Will you run out of money?

This raises a more important question: What is an acceptable starvation probability?

These are all serious questions, and it is quite difficult in this limited space to display all the computer simulations that we conducted. However, you are welcome to visit my website at www.milevsky.com, where the results of many different computer simulations are described at length. And I am not the only one conducting such computer simulations. Various mutual fund companies and other consultants have started performing financial simulations to better forecast your financial future. One particularly good company is Financial Engines, which was founded by Stanford Professor William Sharpe, a Nobel laureate in Economics. I believe that you will be seeing many more computer simulations as people begin to realize the power of this methodology.

CONCLUSION

At the risk of losing the forest for the trees, let me try to summarize what the main points are — and what they are not.

First, there is nothing magical about age 65 as it pertains to asset allocation, exposure to risk, and equity-based mutual funds. At age 65, you can expect to live more than 20, or even 30, years, a time horizon long enough for an exposure to equity. The odds are that you will minimize the probability of starvation with a high allocation to equity, not with term deposits and money market funds. In fact, we saw that a 65-year-old woman who needs to withdraw a fixed annual amount — in our example, 7.5% of her initial wealth — will lower her probability of shortfall from 61.4% to 15.6% by assuming more stock market and equity-based risk. The numbers drop dramatically when you go from 0% equity to 50% equity, but start to decline with even higher levels of equity allocation. Men experience a similar reduction, from 38% to 10%.

From the point of view of pure odds, then, it is very important to have some exposure to equity-based investments, even during your retirement years.

The question, as always, is, how much exposure? What is appropriate for you?

At this point, I must excuse myself and refer you to your licensed financial planner, broker, or investment adviser. No, I am not trying to be lazy or coy.

Indeed, when I am contemplating a personal asset-allocation decision, I try to find the course of action that will maximize the probability of success. But there are so many more aspects to your financial life, such as taxes, estate planning, insurance, debts, and pensions, that I could not possibly provide you with a one-size-fits-all table, or a universal answer to all your asset allocation questions.

My objective is much more modest. It's an attempt to make you think differently about your retirement asset allocation. In fact, if there's one thing you remember from this chapter, I hope it's the following.

When you get financial retirement advice, always be prepared to ask: "What are the odds that I will outlive my money if I follow your suggestions?" If the answer is simply too high for your comfort level, change the plan, or change the planner.

May you live long, and prosper!

C H A P T E R

8

Life Annuities:

It's Not Now or Never

For the most part, baby boomers pay relatively little thought to the eventual payout from their 401(k), IRA, and 403(b) plans, as well as variable annuities and other retirement savings vehicles. Most of us continue to build that hefty nest egg — or rather, carton of eggs — and will worry about how exactly to withdraw from it when the time comes. Our main concern is that it get as large as possible, with as little risk.

But what exactly are the choices once you hit your retirement years?

Well, one way or another, you must turn your investment into a personal retirement pension. In very general terms, you have two distinct choices on how to go about creating this personal pension:

1. you can decide to build and manage your own personal pension; or
2. you can let an insurance company build and manage your personal pension for you.

Now, let me be very clear that the personal pension we are talking about is very distinct from a company pension or government plan, such as social security. With those, you usually have very little choice in the structure of the payout phase, or the payments. You simply retire, go home, and then wait for the monthly check to arrive in the mail.

However, with the personal pensions, such as qualified or non-qualified retirement plans, you can maintain control of the assets and "draw down" the account to fund your retirement needs. The alternative is to hand over (part of) the money to an insurance company and let them send you the monthly checks. The latter option is also known as "annuitization," or buying an immediate life annuity. *An immediate life annuity is very different from a variable annuity (VA).* As discussed in Chapter 4, a VA is a savings vehicle similar to a mutual fund; by contrast, an immediate life annuity is an insurance policy against living too long. More on this later.

If you decide to build your own pension, there is a variety of (messy) tax regulations that stipulate how much you must withdraw every year from your qualified plan, and how much is taxable from the non-qualified plan. And, if you take the annuitization option, you have a myriad of choices from among fixed and variable annuities, as well as guaranteed periods and survivor benefits.

But you see, fundamentally, the two choices are very different. If you decide to annuitize your savings, the insurance company is obligated to send you payments for the rest of your life. Under this choice, you can never outlive your money! On the other hand, if you decide to build your own personal pension (a process I call self-annuitization), there is a serious chance that you will outlive your assets, regardless of your asset mix, as we saw in the previous chapter. I call this longevity risk, the risk that you will live longer than the assets available to support your lifestyle.

The way I look at it, if you decide to buy a life annuity from an insurance company (annuitize), you are transferring the longevity risk to the insurance company. If you decide not to annuitize, you are retaining the longevity risk. But make no mistake about it, longevity risk is real, and should be treated just as seriously as disability, critical illness, and premature death risk. The insurance company is in a far better position than you are to hedge and manage those risks. But, of course, there is a price. And the issue I would like to address in this chapter is whether or not you should self-insure against longevity risk.

My main message is as follows. Life annuities are among the most misunderstood and under-appreciated financial products available in today's marketplace. I believe that most people should have a substantial portion of their retirement assets in life annuities, which I see as financial instruments that insure against longevity risk. And indeed most people are entitled to company pensions and social security, which act as natural longevity insurance. So most people already have large annuities.

On the other hand, despite my unbridled enthusiasm for insuring against longevity risk, it is extremely important that you not annuitize too early in your retirement years. You should try to put it off as long as feasibly possible.

"Why?" you might be asking. "If they are such a great investment (protection) product, should I not buy them as soon as I have the chance?" Well, the main reason is that, for the most part, the purchase of a life annuity is irreversible. Once you've signed the papers, you're committed to that course — for better or worse. My thesis is that, unless there are extenuating circumstances, it makes very little sense for males under the age of 75 or females under the age of 80 to purchase life annuities or to annuitize any additional non-pension wealth. There are two exceptions to this general rule, although both are rare. One is a situation in which long-term interest rates are extraordinarily high. The second may occur if consumers have solid reasons to believe that they are much healthier than the average annuitant. Of course, this is going to be harder for people to judge than whether they are much healthier than other people in the same group.

But, I am getting ahead of myself, so let me start at the beginning — you guessed it, by carefully examining the odds.

First, let's look at how long we are expected to live. According to data provided by the National Center for Health Statistics, the median life span of American males is approximately 75.5 years at birth; for females, it was 82.5 years at birth. But what exactly does this mean? Does it mean that if you are a retired 75-year-old male (or female), you can expect to live less than one (eight) more years in retirement?

Of course, the answer to this question is a resounding no.

The key qualifier here is that the median life span only applies at birth. As you age, your median life span actually increases, so that once you reach retirement, your median life span is longer.

Let me elaborate. The correct way to think about median life is to imagine a group (or, in the language of statisticians, a cohort) of 100,000 baby boys (girls), all born, for the sake of argument, in 1990. And let's assume that we were tracking this large group as they progressed through the human life cycle. Unfortunately, as we know, a small percentage will not survive infancy. Others will succumb to illness or accident in their teenage years, while many more will die in their twenties, thirties, and forties.

With the help of actuaries and demographers, the National

Center for Health Statistics estimates that in 75.5 years (82.5 for females), only 50,000 individuals will be left from the original group of 100,000. Half the group will have died prior to age 75.5 (82.5). In other words, males and females at birth have a 50% chance of reaching age 75.5 and 82.5 respectively.

However, if you are still alive at age 70, you have a greater than 50/50 chance of living out the full statistical term. That's because at 70, you have already survived many potentially fatal illnesses, maladies, and accidents.

The numbers confirm this. In fact, if we were to perform the experiment slightly differently and track a cohort of 100,000 males (females) who were 70 years old in 1990, many more than 50,000 would still be alive by age 75.5 (82.5). For this particular cohort of 70-year-olds, half would survive to the ripe old age of 81.5 (85.5). We can therefore state that the median life span for a 70-year-old male (female) is 81.5 (85.5), which is roughly six (three) years more than the equivalent numbers at birth.

As Table 8.1 indicates, this process continues at ages 75, 80, 85, and so on.

Table 8.1

Median Life Span at Different Ages

Current Age	Female	Male
55	83.5	77.5
65	84.5	78.5
70	85.5	81.5
75	86.5	83.5
80	88.5	86.5
85	91.0	89.5
90	94.0	93.5
95	97.5	97.5

(Source: U.S. Decennial Life Tables for 1989–1991, Centers for Disease Control and Prevention)

It's also interesting to note that, as you age, the gap between males and females decreases. By age 95, both males and females have between two and three years left to live on average. Moreover, the rate at which median life expectancy increases accelerates at age 65. Prior to that age, the numbers are relatively flat, with most deaths occurring in the early years of life.

An analogy that I find helpful is to imagine an unbiased roulette wheel in a casino. The odds of the ball landing on red or black in any particular spin of the wheel are exactly 50/50, so the odds of landing on red six times in a row are $(0.5)^6$, which is about 1.5% — very small, I would say. In other words, it's a pretty safe bet that you will not see a six-red episode.

But if you have already spun the wheel five times, and they all came up red, the odds of the next (the sixth) spin being red are still 50/50. This is a manifestation of what is known as "event conditioning"; once you have more information, the *conditional* odds change. Put another way, the odds of getting six reds in a row depend on how many reds you have seen already.

Table 8.2 should give you a sense of what the actual probabilities are like, in the context of human mortality. I have chosen age 65 as the standard baseline for retirement, although similar numbers can be generated for any age.

As you can see, a male aged 65 stands a 29.5% chance — a bit less than one in three — of actually reaching age 85. That means, of course, that he'd be spending 20 years of his life in retirement. A 65-year-old female stands a 47.9% chance — a bit less than one in two — of reaching age 85. In fact, there's an astonishing 27.8% chance (better than one in four) that a 65-year-old female will live until age 90 and spend 25 years in retirement.

This means, once again, that from today's cohort of

Table 8.2

What are the chances of living to various ages?

(Current age is 65)

Live-to Age	Female	Male
70	92.7%	86.6%
75	81.9%	69.5%
80	66.8%	49.6%
85	47.9%	29.5%
90	27.8%	13.3%
95	11.4%	3.9%

(Source: U.S. Decennial Life Tables for 1989–1991, Centers for Disease Control and Prevention)

100,000 65-year-old females, 27,800 are likely to still be around in 25 more years. In the same manner, 11.4%, or 11,400, are likely to be alive in 30 years.

One final, interesting exercise is to take a married couple, where both the man and the woman are 65 years old, and estimate the chances that at least one will still be alive at age 90. This will give you a sense of how to budget for couples as opposed to individuals.

Here's how the calculation is performed. There are, of course, four possibilities: Event #1 — both are dead by age 90; Event #2 — both are alive at age 90; Event #3 — the husband is alive and the wife is dead at age 90; and Event #4 — the wife is alive and the husband is dead at age 90. Mathematically, the probabilities of these four events must add up to 100%. In other words, (Probability of Event #1) + (Probability of Event #2) + (Probability of Event #3) + (Probability of Event #4) = 100%.

To calculate the chances that at least one of them will live to 90, then, we simply have to subtract from 100% the probability that both will die by age 90 (Event #1). Then we will be left with the sum of the probabilities of the three events we are interested in: both husband and wife are alive (#2); the husband is alive and the wife is dead (#3); and, the wife is alive and the husband is dead (#4).

This means that 100% – (PE#1) = (PE#2) + (PE#3) + (PE#4). The odds that neither of them survive (PE#1) are calculated by multiplying the odds of the wife not surviving to 90 (which we can figure from Table 8.2 to be 1 – 0.278) by the odds of the husband not surviving (1 – 0.133). The result is (1 – 0.278) x (1 – 0.133) = 0.626, which is a 62.6% chance. So when we subtract the probabilities of neither surviving from 100%, we get 100% – 62.6% = 37.4%. Therefore, 37.4% is the probability that at least one will survive to age 90. Contrast that with the wife's and husband's individual chances of living to age 90 (27.8% and 13.3%, respectively); the idea is that with high certainty, at least one will get to that age.

Of course, I should mention that some actuaries and demographers have documented the existence of a "broken heart" effect which tends to increase the odds, just slightly, of one spouse dying just after the other has passed away. So, to be very precise, I should say that the above calculation assumes complete independence between the two events.

But, of much more importance is the fact that the numbers in Table 8.2 represent an average across all socioeconomic levels of American society. As such, they are probably a downward-biased estimate of how long you will live. As many studies have shown, wealth and health are correlated. By the mere fact that you are reading this book, you are probably wealthier and healthier than average. This is known in the insurance industry as "adverse selection" — meaning that people who buy life annuities tend to live longer than average. As we shall see, insurance companies are well aware of this phenomenon and often adjust their annuity prices to reverse the implications of the self-selection process.

Now that we have seen how long people are living in retirement, let's look at how the insurance companies use that information to price annuities.

How does an annuity work? In its most general form, purchasing a life annuity (whether joint, fixed-term, or single) involves paying a non-refundable lump sum to an insurance company in exchange for a guaranteed monthly or quarterly income.

With some products, the income ends after a pre-determined or fixed period of time; these are called fixed-term (or period-certain) annuities. With life annuities, the income ends with death. Obviously, a person cannot outlive the income from a life annuity; this is one of the product's strong selling points. No matter how long you live, how markets perform, or what happens to interest rates or the economy as a whole, you will always get a monthly check. (Unless, of course, the company becomes insolvent, in which case your state insurance commissioner's office will take over.)

Life annuities, in other words, are a type of longevity insurance — the exact opposite of traditional life insurance. We buy annuities because we are afraid of living too long and will need income to support those extra years of life. We buy life insurance because we are afraid of dying too soon and leaving family and loved ones in financial need.

Insurance companies can provide this lifelong benefit by (a) pooling a large enough group of annuitants and (b) making a very careful and conservative assumption about the rate of return earned on its assets. The pooling of annuitants means that individuals who do not reach their life expectancy, as calculated by actuarial mortality tables, will end up subsidizing those who exceed it.

As Table 8.3 suggests, in the current interest-rate environment — and these numbers may change on a weekly

Table 8.3

Sample Annuity Quotes

($100,000 buys monthly payments for life)

Current Age	Female	Male
55	$533	$591
65	$630	$730
70	$712	$844
75	$832	$1,008
80	$1,014	$1,250

(Source: See Notes section)

basis — a 65-year-old single female with $100,000 can purchase an annuity that will provide her with $630 per month for the rest of her life, no matter how long she lives. The same $100,000 will buy an annuity that will provide a male with the greater amount of $730 per month for life. The additional $100 per month, or 16%, that a male will receive is a direct result of his lower life expectancy.

Remember that our cohort of 65-year-old men can expect to live 14 more years; our cohort of 65-year-old females, on the other hand, can expect to live 20 more years, on average. If the money must last for longer, the payments must be smaller.

You can therefore view a life annuity as a bet with the insurance company. You are betting (and hoping) that you will exceed your cohort's median life span; they are betting (and perhaps hoping) that you will not. Of course, they wish you personally no harm, but your prolonged health is definitely not their first priority.

Of course, I may be guilty of emphasizing the adversarial nature of the relationship over the valuable social function performed by the company as an intermediary that pools risks. But I am simply trying to illustrate that there is a gamble implicit in the purchase of a life annuity, just as there is with life insurance.

With that in mind, if the 65-year-old exceeds the median life span of approximately 14 (20) more years, he (she) will have won the bet, and will end up earning a return that is greater than the average interest rate that applied at the time of purchase. If he or she falls short of the median life span, the return will be inferior.

One further important fact to note is that insurance actuaries use mortality tables that are biased toward a much longer life. They do not really use National Center for Health Statistics tables to calculate life expectancy and mortality probabilities; they use tables that assume people live longer than the population average.

Table 8.4

How long do insurance companies (annuity vendors) think you are going to live?

(Current age is 65)

Live-to age:	Female	Male
70	95%	92%
75	89%	82%
80	78%	67%
85	62%	49%
90	40%	30%
95	19%	14%

(Source: Society of Actuaries, 1996 Individual Annuity Mortality table)

When you compare these numbers to Table 8.2, the differences are remarkable. The insurance actuaries believe that your probability of survival until age 85 is 62% for females and 49% for males. Compare this to the population tables, where the number is 47.9% for females and 29.5% for males. So which is it then? What are the *true* odds of living for 20 more years? Why is there such a big difference in estimates?

This, again, is known as adverse selection or, more

affectionately, the "lemon problem." The reason that used cars sell for much less than newer ones is because buyers are suspicious of the motives of sellers and demand a lower price to compensate for the uncertainty. (In other words, is the car being sold because it's a lemon?)

In a similar fashion, insurance companies are wary of people who are willing to bet that they will live longer than the average. (Do the buyers of annuities know something that the insurance company doesn't? Is grandma still alive at 102?) To mitigate the mortality risk, they therefore price the life annuity with the healthiest people in mind.

Stretching the imagination, we might compare purchasing a life annuity to an all-you-can-eat buffet at your favorite restaurant. Initially, it always seems like a good deal because you can eat as much as you want. "What a bargain," you think to yourself. "I can eat as much as I want at a fixed price."

But think again. The restaurant owners know what they are doing. The buffet is priced to take into account the eating habits and capacity of the average diner. Furthermore, the restaurant will factor in the principle of adverse selection. Chances are, if you choose the buffet, you are hungrier than average — and you're thinking that you'll get a better deal because you will be eating so much. The only way you "win the bet" on the buffet is if you eat more than the average consumer. But remember: we are not just talking about any average consumer; we are talking about the average consumer who actually chooses the buffet.

Another interesting aspect of life annuities is that the monthly payments that you can receive increase the longer you wait before buying the annuity. As noted, for example, a 65-year-old male (female) can get $730 ($630) per month from a $100,000 annuity. But if they waited another 10 years to make the purchase, until age 75, the male (female) would get $1,008 ($832), for life. That's an increase of approximately 35%, simply for deferring the purchase for 10 years.

What's the catch? Once again, median life span is the key. At age 75, a man's median life span is 83.5 years (86.5 for women). This translates into an average of 9 (12) more years of payments, as opposed to 14 (20) more years when you annuitize at age 65. The fewer years the age cohort is likely to live, the larger the monthly payments will be. So the lesson is that the longer you wait, the more you will get per month.

Of course, we are cheating a bit because we are comparing apples and oranges. If you annuitize at age 65, you start receiving your monthly check immediately, whereas if you wait for 10 years, you won't receive any payments during that period. And if you need to withdraw and consume funds from the $100,000, you will then have less than $100,000 left in 10 years' time. I'll come back to this point later on.

There are alternatives to life annuities. The natural one is the do-it-yourself annuity. In the life insurance lexicon, consumers are familiar with the idea that it's often a good strategy to "buy term and invest the difference." The premise of this approach is that investors can earn a better rate of return than the insurer will pay and should therefore only purchase the pure insurance component.

As you probably know, there are two basic categories of life insurance. The first one is called whole-life (also known as permanent, or cash-value) insurance and the second major category is known as term insurance. Whole-life consists of a savings component and an insurance component. Term, on the other hand, simply consists of an insurance component — and obviously costs less in annual premiums. The reason people tend to buy (more expensive) whole-life insurance is because they would like to save money for the future. (Or for the more jaded reader, because insurance is sold, not purchased.) Insurance companies bundle the savings and insurance components into one annual premium. It's like buying a fax and printer in one. Maybe it saves space. Maybe it saves money.

The point is, in this context, that individuals are usually counseled to buy term insurance and manage their own savings themselves.

Similarly, you can manage — or create — your own annuity. For example, the retiring 65-year-old male (female) can keep the $100,000 invested in an IRA for the next few years and then start withdrawing a fixed monthly income of exactly $730 ($630). That, you will remember, is the hypothetical annuity amount that the insurance company would have provided at age 65. (As far as taxes are concerned, the entire $730 will be subject to ordinary income tax rates, regardless of the source of the funds.) But what if you live too long? Will your money last? It's true that this do-it-yourself strategy runs a serious financial risk: underfunding retirement in the event of long-run inferior investment returns in conjunction with unexpected human longevity.

Here's my compromise solution and recommended strategy: a modification I call the "do-it-yourself-and-then-switch-if-you-want" strategy. It offers some great odds. Here's how it works. The qualified plan is depleted at the same rate as a hypothetical life annuity would have provided. Then, after a number of years, the retiree collapses the plan and purchases a life annuity. (Technically, this can only be done if you have chosen to take the minimum distributions from a qualified plan, under the annually recalculated life expectancy.)

My thinking runs as follows. At retirement, you can continue to invest your savings and easily beat the mortality-adjusted rate of return from a life annuity, while withdrawing, to meet living expenses, exactly the same amount that a hypothetical annuity would have provided. Then, in about 10 or 15 years, you have a very good chance of being able to acquire precisely the same $730 ($630)-per-month life annuity, using your remaining wealth.

So what exactly are the odds of success here? What are the chances that you can purchase precisely the same $730 ($630)-per-month life annuity in the future by following this do-it-yourself-and-then-switch strategy?

Here are some numbers. I'll explain in a minute how I arrived at them.

1. A 65-year-old male (female) keeps the $100,000 in his or her qualified plan, such as an IRA, and invests the money in a diversified portfolio, instead of buying a life annuity from an insurance company.

2. At the same time, the male (female) sets up a systematic plan to withdraw $730 ($630) per month, for the next 5, 10, or 15 years. This $730 ($630) per month, remember, is not arbitrary. Rather, it is the hypothetical amount that a life annuity would have provided at age 65. (This is known as self-annuitization.)

3. In 5, 10, or 15 years, the remaining funds in the portfolio — the exact amount of which will depend on how the investments have performed during that period — are used to purchase a life annuity from an insurance company.

4. If the monthly annuity that results is greater than $730 ($630), we can say that the deferral of the annuity purchase was successful. If the monthly annuity that results is less than $730 ($630), then we would have to conclude that the deferral was a failure.

As Table 8.5 shows, a 65-year-old male (female) has an 87% (91%) chance of being able to purchase the exact same

Table 8.5

Probability of Successful Deferral

(Individual age is 65)

Deferral Period	Female	Male
5 years	91%	87%
10 years	93%	89%
15 years	94%	90%

(Source: Author's estimates; see Notes section)

annuity five years from now. He (she) has an 89% (93%) chance of being able to purchase the exact same life annuity 10 years from now.

The odds for the male, you will note, are slightly lower than for the female. Why? Simply because the do-it-yourself part involves a higher level of consumption, which naturally leaves less funds for investment.

You might be asking yourself "Where in the world did he get those numbers? How does he know that those are the odds? How does he know if I'll have enough to buy the life annuity in 5, 10, or 15 years?"

These are all very good questions. Let me try to explain.

As you may recall, one of the main themes in this book is that your financial future is random, uncertain, and unpredictable. So any financial projections that ignore the uncertainty — or that don't tell you the odds — are giving you half the picture at best. However, although it is impossible to predict, you can ask questions, and get meaningful answers, about your financial future by using Monte Carlo computer simulations. The computer simulations can give you the probability of regret from choosing various courses of action. These are the same kind of simulations I described in the Introduction and in Chapter 7. In Chapter 7 I was focusing on the question of a suitable mix between stocks and bonds; this time I am looking at the annuity question. Specifically, to get the probability of regret on the deferral strategy, I simulated millions of individuals — at various ages — who all withdraw the fixed amount the annuity would have provided each and every month. After running these scenarios, and looking at how much money people had left after 5, 10, 15, and 20 years, I counted the number of scenarios in which they had enough to buy the exact same life annuity they originally contemplated. Sometimes they didn't have enough to buy the same life annuity, but — overwhelmingly — most times they did.

This Monte Carlo computer simulation was somewhat trickier than in the retirement asset allocation case, mainly because I had to keep track of two different things. First of all, I had to monitor each individual's wealth over the next 20 years. But I also had to keep track of exactly how much the insurance companies were likely to charge for life annuities during the next 20 years. This more complicated exercise involved making assumptions about mortality patterns, insurance loads, and interest rates. If you're interested in these details, see the end-of-chapter notes at the back of this book for references.

The computer simulation sounds complex, and it is, but it is still possible to understand intuitively exactly *why* it is that if you defer your annuity purchase for 5, 10, or even 15 years, you probably will have enough money left over to buy exactly the same product you could buy today. I'll try to explain in a couple of different ways, but please bear in mind that in my explanation I'm going to assume that interest rates will remain constant at 5%, just to make things easier to understand.

First, let's revisit Table 8.3, with its sample annuity quotes, and use the numbers in a slightly different way. If a 65-year-old female gets a monthly $630 from her $100,000 annuity purchase, then she has paid roughly $100,000 divided by (12 x $630) = $13.23 for each $1 of lifetime yearly income.

Similarly, if a 75-year-old female gets a monthly $832 from her $100,000 annuity, then she has paid about $100,000 divided by (12 x $832) = $10.02 for each $1 of lifetime yearly income. As you can quickly see, this yearly income — with a lifetime guarantee — becomes $3.21 "cheaper" if the 65-year-old female waits 10 more years before buying the annuity.

Why is it cheaper? Because the 75-year-old has less time left in the human life cycle compared with the 65-year-old. The same amount of money, $100,000, returned with interest over a shorter period of time, translates into more money per month.

But, in fact, it's not just cheaper by $3.21, because we are comparing prices across 10 different years. Because of inflation and the time-value of money, that $10.02 10 years from now would be worth a lot less than $10.02 today. So to get a better sense of how much "cheaper" the annuity will be if you waited 10 years, you must subtract the present value of $10.02 ($6.15 when the interest rate is 5%) from the current price of $13.23. Stated differently, if you invested $6.15 for 10 years at 5% per annum, you would have exactly $10.02 in 10 years. So the true measure of how much cheaper the annuity would become by waiting 10 years is $13.23 – $6.15 = $7.08.

But the $7.08 is for each dollar of income per year. Now let's convert back to the original numbers. You'll recall that the $630 per month that a female can obtain from a life annuity purchased at age 65 translates into 12 x $630 = $7,560 per year. Therefore, by waiting 10 years, she would "save" $7.08 x $7,560 = $53,525 from her initial wealth of $100,000.

I use the word "save" in conjunction with the sum of $53,525 because it represents the amount from the $100,000 that you don't need in order to buy the annuity in 10 years. You only need the remaining $46,475.

Of course, we must be careful here not to abuse the word "save." If you annuitize today, at age 65, you earn monthly payments of $630 for life, starting immediately. On the other hand, if you annuitize in 10 years, at age 75, you don't receive the $630 monthly payments during the next decade. So you're not really saving $53,525, because you'll surely need to draw on some of those funds in order to live until the annuity is purchased. There is, in other words, no free lunch.

Still, if you can invest the $53,525 and successfully withdraw $630 per month for the next 10 years, then it is worthwhile to wait before you annuitize. This is not a personal decision about whether you can live on $630 per month; rather, it's a matter of whether you can invest your money and earn a higher return than the insurance company is implicitly giving you during the next 10 years.

So when I speak of "successful" withdrawal, I mean that you are able to earn a high enough rate of return on your $53,525 so that, consuming that $630 per month, you do not exhaust your funds before the end of the 10-year period. Remember, you are actually investing the entire $100,000. But the remaining $46,475 (invested in relatively safe assets) has been mentally set aside for the annuity purchase in 10 years' time. In sum, you are living on $53,525 for the next 10 years.

Obviously, financial success and failure has a probability attached to it, and that is exactly what I am trying to compute. I'm examining the odds that you can bake your own annuity — consuming the same $630 every month — and still have enough left over to buy the annuity, if you so desire, later on in the life cycle.

I am advocating that you mentally split your initial capital of $100,000 into two parts. The first part, $53,525, you will invest and live on for the next 10 years. The second part, the remaining $46,475, you will ideally place in an investment that is negatively correlated with interest rates — so that you can purchase your annuity in 10 years' time.

In practice, the negative correlation simply means that you put the $46,475 in an investment that is more likely to appreciate the lower interest rates get (even though in this simple example, I assumed that rates are constant at 5%). A balanced portfolio of common equities and long-term bonds provides a good example of investments that would increase in value if interest rates fall. In this manner, if annuity payouts decrease during the next 10 years, your portfolio will increase in value, and you'll be able to afford exactly the same annuity stream.

Of course, this is where the probability argument comes in — and why I had to conduct the Monte Carlo computer simulation. What are the odds that you will be able to withdraw $630 per month — for the next 10 years — from your $53,525 without depleting it? Similarly, what are the odds that the remaining $46,475 can be invested so that you can buy exactly the same annuity in 10 years? The numbers in Table 8.5 seem to indicate high odds.

Table 8.6

If you purchase a life annuity with $100,000, what is your IRR, assuming you live to age 95?

Purchase Age	Female	Male
65	6.66%	8.24%
75	8.22%	11.17%
80	9.37%	13.54%
85	10.00%	19.62%

(Source: Annuity values from Table 8.3)

I promised two ways to intuitively understand the computer results. Here is an additional explanation for why it is so much more appealing and logical to annuitize at age 75 or 80 rather than at age 65. Table 8.6 is a supplement to

Table 8.3. It shows the internal rate of return (IRR) — a measure of profitability — from purchasing a life annuity with $100,000 at various ages, assuming that you will live and receive payments until age 95.

Table 8.6 states that if an 80-year-old male purchases a life annuity, and survives to age 95 — thus receiving $1,250 per month for 15 years — he will earn an implicit 13.54% annual return on his initial investment. It is implicit because when you discount 15 years of $1,250 monthly payments, at a rate of 13.54% per year, you obtain the original $100,000. (Think of it like a $100,000 home mortgage amortized at 13.54% over a 15-year period, with monthly payments of $1,250.)

The same purchase at age 85 provides an even better yield — an implicit 19.62% annual return. A 19.62% return is very high and would clearly be difficult to beat using alternative investment classes. However, at age 65, the internal rate of return is much lower (8.24%), even with the assumption that you live to age 95.

This 8.24%, then, becomes your threshold. If you can earn that return, or greater, using alternative investment vehicles, then it's worthwhile to wait. If you can't beat the 8.24% — with reasonable probability — then you should buy the annuity. Therefore, another reason for deferring the decision to annuitize — retaining the option to eventually annuitize — is that the implicit rate of return is quite low to begin with, at age 65, but becomes virtually impossible to beat, at later ages, using alternative investment classes.

Of course, some caveats are in order. First, there is no guarantee that annuity prices for a 75-year-old will remain — in the example of the 75-year-old female — at $832 per $100,000, or in other words at $10.02 per $1 of lifetime yearly income. In fact, the $832 could decrease (and thus the $10.02 may increase), if interest rates were to decline over the next 10 years. That's why I am more likely to advocate this deferral strategy in a low-interest-rate environment, where the probability of further reductions over the next 10 years is small.

Second, to the detriment of the buyer, even without a decline in interest rates, insurance companies may decide to change their mortality assumptions to incorporate longer life spans, thus reducing the monthly payment. However, I believe that this particular risk is outweighed by the probability of illness, and the value of keeping your options open; naturally, people who become ill soon after making the irrevocable decision to buy the annuity will regret their decision.

It is very important to stress that this strategy only works if the funds you will later use to buy the annuity are invested in a well-diversified way. Putting the funds in a low-interest-bearing bank deposit defeats the point, and would likely make it impossible to ever purchase the same annuity in the future. In our previous example, the $7.08 must be invested using a high allocation to equity in order to generate the $1 per year for 10 years.

The flip side to this argument is the incredible value that comes from annuitizing at older ages, when the individual may not be concerned with leaving an estate. Take the 80-year-old male in Table 8.3, for example. He earns $1,250 per month for every $100,000. This implies a cost of $100,000 divided by (12 x $1,250) = $6.67 for every $1 of yearly lifetime income. It is difficult to generate that kind of return from conventional instruments.

Of course, an obvious question to ask about this approach is, why bother? What's the purpose of not buying a life annuity now if you're going to buy it in 10 years and withdraw the same amount each month anyway? Why bother with an elaborate strategy that may not even work?

The answer to this question is twofold. First, you as the

retiree maintain complete control over your funds, which means that your liquidity is maintained. Thus, any emergency or unforeseen cash crunch, especially for long-term care, can be met from the non-annuitized pool. Second, you retain the option to annuitize at any time. Why pay for something today if, in all probability, you can pay for it in 10 years with no real increase in cost, and no diminishment in the benefits of the purchase?

An additional factor is inflation. Most of today's annuities are largely inadequate in protecting against inflation. (There are annuities available that protect you from inflation — so-called "real annuities" — but they are relatively more expensive.) There is also a very good chance that future annuity products will offer attractive features that do not exist today, such as commutability (the ability to cash in the product for a portion of your money back). Maintaining control of the funds allows you to hedge the inflation risk by purchasing assets that tend to increase in inflationary periods. Annuitization is akin to purchasing a bond with amortized principal and souped-up coupons. The coupons are higher than normal because the bond is completely non-transferable and goes with you to the grave. As many of us have learned the hard way, unexpected inflation — together with a general increase in interest rates — will wreak havoc on bond prices. The same thing goes for annuities.

Even though they are not traded in the marketplace, annuities still lose theoretical value when interest rates increase. Those who think that inflation is permanently dead should ask themselves why the spread between yields on real and nominal bonds is at 2%–3%. In other words, very roughly speaking, investors are expecting at least 2%–3% inflation per year, over the next 30 years. This means that, at 2%, your $730 ($630) per month will only be worth half as much, in today's dollars, 30 years from now. And if our 65-year-old couple doesn't worry that far ahead, then he (and she) shouldn't be purchasing a life annuity in the first place. So, if you're going to worry, you might as well do it right.

There is one additional reason for deferring (and perhaps even avoiding, in some cases) the decision to annuitize as long as prudently possible — the bequest motive. Purchasing a pure life annuity will leave nothing for the estate. Remember that with a straight life annuity, payments cease with your death. The worst-case scenario, which many people fear, is that you hand over $100,000 to the insurance company, which promises you monthly checks for the rest of your life; then, a few months later, you die. The monthly checks stop coming, the remaining portion of the $100,000 rightfully belongs to the insurance company, and your estate is left with nothing. If there is a guarantee period, which of course you pay for, the monthly payments will continue until the guarantee period is over. So in that sense, the estate, children, or loved ones will get something.

Nevertheless, the whole idea of annuity purchases involves the pooling of risk. The living are subsidized by the dying. In fact, participants of qualified retirement plans must obtain written permission from their spouses in order to elect a single-life annuity payment option.

With this in mind, the longer you can defer annuitization, the greater the chances — morbid though this may sound — that you will die prior to purchasing the life annuity. That means your estate inherits the proceeds of the account. Taxes will complicate things, but marginal tax rates are still far less than 100%, so there will always be something left over.

CONCLUSION

Contemporary economics has developed a technique known as option pricing theory. One of the things it teaches us is that having the right — but not the obligation — to buy something is valuable and should be exercised, with appropriate caution. A decision that is irreversible (like buying a life annuity) should only be undertaken when the potential value of keeping the option alive is worth less than the immediate benefit of exercising the option. That, for example, is why exchange-traded stock options are rarely exercised early.

The same concept applies to the irreversible purchase of a life annuity. For the most part, a qualified plan can always be converted to annuities, but annuities can never be converted back to systematic withdrawals. For individuals who are willing to tolerate a minimal probability of shortfall, it therefore makes very little sense in my judgment to annuitize in your sixties and early seventies. The odds say that it makes more sense to wait. But, at some point, make sure to have some longevity insurance. The risk will eventually creep up on you!

CHAPTER

9

No Regrets:

What Is a Risky Future?

I want to conclude with a question: How do you define financial risk? Do you see it as synonymous with price volatility, market fluctuations, terrifying headlines, and day-to-day uncertainty? One week the New York Stock Exchange average gains 5%; the next week, it loses 10%. One quarter, your mutual fund earns 27% — wonderful. But the next quarter, it loses 34% — not so wonderful. Is this what financial risk means to you? If it is, then national and international stock markets — especially given the volatility of 1998 — are definitely places to avoid.

And you wouldn't be alone. For bureaucrats, corporate executives, central bankers, elected politicians, and even mutual fund managers, market turmoil is also a very risky business. In many cases, their lucrative jobs may be at stake. These people have to be seen trying to do something. Often, they are damned if they do and damned if they don't.

Take a look at Figure 9.1. It seems to conform to the volatility view of financial risk. It shows — side by side — the month-over-month (after-inflation) returns from the U.S. stock market and three-month treasury bills. For every year since 1950, it indicates how much you would have earned from investing your money in treasury bills and how much you would have earned from a diversified portfolio in the U.S. stock market.

So you tell me, which asset class is risky and which asset class is safe? If market fluctuations are your preferred measure of risk, then the answer is a no-brainer. Equity markets will take you on a wild and volatile ride. They are, in that sense, risky. Short-term debt instruments, on the other hand, are safe. Safe means stable. It means year-to-year predictability. It means no surprises.

However, for individuals facing personal financial decisions (namely, all of us), I'm not convinced that volatility and fluctuations capture the true measure of financial risk. To me, financial risk is something much more intuitive and definitive than some jagged lines generated on a well-designed graph.

Figure 9.1 Monthly Returns: U.S. Stock Market vs. T-Bills 1950–1999

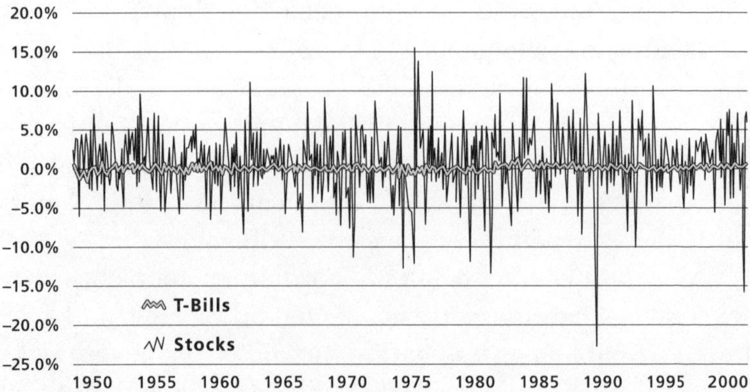

Financial decision making, as we saw in the Introduction, has much to learn from the science of weather forecasting. Issues of financial risk, I submit, should be framed and explained in terms of what I have called the Probability of Regret (PoR). Financial risk is the probability that you will look back — with 20/20 hindsight — and regret the original decision. Financial risk is measured by the probability that you could or would have done better by simply going with the safe, risk-free solution.

If you are willing to accept shortfall regret as the relevant risk in your life — and this may not be easy — then financial risk has an embedded dimension of time. It is meaningless to talk about risk without also talking about an appropriate time horizon over which you are contemplating the investment decision.

Is the stock market risky? Well, that depends. Using only a short-term horizon, it's absolutely risky. Using a long-term horizon, I would argue that most equity markets probably are not. Are treasury bills, savings bonds, and term deposits safe? Well, once again, that depends on time. In the short term, they're the safest things available. After all, they are implicitly guaranteed by federal and provincial authorities. Their returns are reliable and predictable. But, in the same manner, I would argue that over the long term, such investments are risky.

How can that be? If it's safe to hold a guaranteed savings bond for one year, why is it risky to hold it for 10? Once again, it comes down to how you feel about risk. If you're like me, and you consider risk to be the probability of regret (PoR), then I believe that in the long run, you will regret the decision to invest in these instruments because the other asset classes will do better. The odds that equity markets will perform worse than these apparently safe instruments decline exponentially over time.

The longer you own the equity asset class, the lower will

be your probability of regret. The longer you hold the equity asset class, the lower the odds that you will look back and say, "Oh, what a mistake I made!" Look back at the chart in the Introduction: the shortfall risk of regret declines as the time horizon lengthens.

Of course, I am not counseling recklessness. Caution is warranted here. And I'm certainly not dismissing the importance of short-term deposits and money market funds. They are the only vehicles to use — the only place to park your money — if your goals are strictly short term. Perhaps you're planning to buy a house in a few years, and are saving for a downpayment. Perhaps your car has an overdue appointment with the wrecker, and you're saving for a new one. Perhaps you want a new boat or a new cottage or even a new dining room set. These are short-horizon objectives; the money to fund these needs should only be placed in short-term, risk-free guaranteed instruments. Those who ignored — or plan to ignore — this advice should think back to the capital-eroding third quarter of 1998 or early 2000. Short-term money has no place in a long-term game.

All your investment adviser, financial planner, or stockbroker can do is give you the odds — the probability of regret. But only you can decide whether to take an umbrella.

So how long should you plan for? What is your time horizon? How long are you likely to live and what are the odds of reaching that age? Chapter 8 gave us a very good indication of the probabilities of reaching various ages. As I argued, the odds of living into your eighties or nineties are today quite favorable. Remember, it's not just the median life span — or the average — that matters. It's the odds of reaching advanced ages.

More important, it's not just your physical time horizon that matters; your mental time horizon is even more crucial. In fact, it's your mental horizon that will determine how much risk you can bear.

Do you have a short- or a long-term mental horizon? How can you tell? Well, do you wake up at 3:00 a.m. worrying about how the Japanese markets are doing and how they will affect the next day's trading on North American markets? Is the mutual fund section of your daily newspaper the first thing you look at with your morning coffee? Is your Internet browser set to four different websites that give you up-to-the-minute values on your investments? Do you hang up on your spouse when your broker calls?

If your answer to any of the above is yes, then I would venture to guess that you certainly don't have a long-term investment horizon. You may claim to be investing for the long run, but that's just lip service. Your daily actions contradict that dispassionate, I'm-here-for-the-duration philosophy. You are basically acting like a myopic short-term investor.

What's the difference between long and short term? What happens in the long term that is so different from the year-over-year behavior? Compare Figure 9.1 with Figure 9.2. In Figure 9.2, you see the cumulative (after-inflation) results of investing one dollar in the equity markets and one dollar in the treasury bill markets from 1950 until 1999. Look at the gap. Look at the margin. Where is the place to

Figure 9.2 Real Value of One Dollar Invested in 1950 (T-Bills vs. Equity)

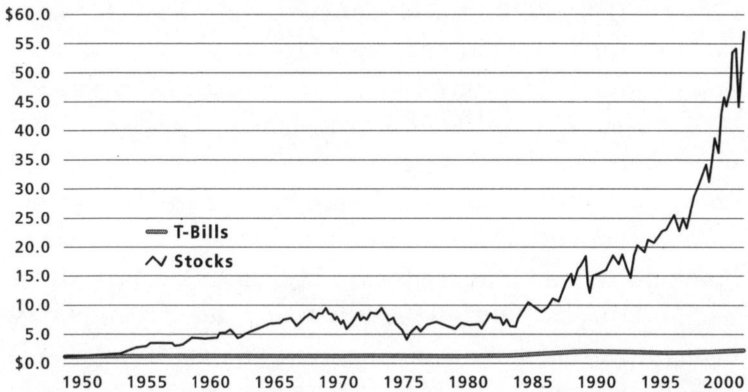

be — after all is said and done — and which investment would you regret?

Figure 9.1 seems to contradict Figure 9.2. In Figure 9.1, equities seem historically the riskier asset class, their behavior volatile, unpredictable, and uncertain. Yet in Figure 9.2, equities completely beat treasury bills. So are equity markets safe, or are they risky? Well, here we go again. It all comes down to time horizon. In the long term, the risk declines. In the long term, the risk is mitigated. Why is that so? Why should equity markets go up in the long term? Why should they beat the performance of other asset classes? Why should they give you the best odds? What's the catch? Why should I be rewarded — just for waiting? How do we know that the past is any indication of the future? True, for the last 50 years, the risk of equity investments declined over time. But who says the next 50 years will mirror that pattern?

It all comes down to risk and reward. If you're willing to live with short-term risk — willing to tolerate short-term fluctuations and day-to-day volatility — you will be compensated in the long run. If you can't handle the short term, if the uncertainty is stressful and the headlines are unbearable, then the markets are too hot for you: get out of the kitchen. You don't have the right horizon. You don't have the right risk profile. You don't have the right psychological makeup for stock market exposure. At the same time, of course, you will not be entitled to the long-term rewards.

But what if your neighbor or broker gives you a hot, can't-miss stock tip? What if you hear about a wonderful new high-tech company that's just about to go public with its first share offering? What if you read about a great new stock in the newspaper? Inevitably, these kinds of things happen. But I would ask: Is this really the way to choose equity investments?

You may think you're getting in on the ground floor,

before the rest of the investment world has discovered your new jewel. In all likelihood, you're wrong. This, I would argue, is a mug's game. It's a waste of money and, more important, it will mean a loss of future confidence in the stock market when you realize that the stock has fizzled, or has failed to keep pace with the broader market. Remember, you are competing against thousands of highly skilled analysts who spend their days — and much of their nights — poring over financial statements and annual reports looking for the next big hit. Count on it: you will be out-numbered, out-smarted, and out-maneuvered by the competition. Stick to your day job.

Yes, your golfing buddy, good old Chuck, bought a stock that tripled in a week. But did he tell you about all the tip-based investments he made that went nowhere? This is survivorship bias. You only hear about the winners. So it doesn't matter if this company is on the verge of inventing a perpetual motion machine that will change the world. Just ask yourself this question: "What edge do I have? What gives me better odds than anybody else playing this game?" If you can identify the edge — and it's legal — then go ahead; by all means, take the plunge. Otherwise, stick to investing, not speculating. Remember, if it sounds too good to be true, you haven't been listening carefully.

Although I hate rules of thumb — especially when it comes to money and finance — here is one I feel pretty comfortable with. If somebody promises you more than a 30% return on your stock, mutual fund, or limited partnership investment in one year — without any risk to your principal — hang up the phone and call the Securities and Exchange Commission (SEC).

And let me add this: By singling out 30% as ridiculous, I'm not saying that 25% is a reasonable expectation of profit. All I'm saying is that at the 30% level, you must be taking some very serious risks. Most likely, there is leverage lurking there somewhere and, as you will recall from Chapter 6, the downside of leverage can be ugly.

So let's say I've convinced you. What next? Do you call your broker and ask him or her to buy you a couple of good stocks? Pick a few solid companies with decent dividend yields and sturdy business prospects? Or should you go to mutual funds? And if mutual funds are the preferred route, how should you pick one from the scores available?

These questions lead us to the importance of diversification, both national and international (Chapter 5). It's not the number of investments that count; it's how (or whether) they move together that matters. Buying 10 stocks or 10 mutual funds can be just as risky as buying one stock or one fund, if they are all in the same general economic and financial sector. Remember, it's the correlation that counts. Yes, they all should go up over time, but when one investment zigs, you want the other investment to zag. You want to own enough stocks, bonds, etc. to reduce, as much as possible, the probability that you will regret that investment.

In fact, the concept of correlation goes far beyond your simple investment portfolio. It's not just investments in financial capital that should be constructed with low correlation. Investments in your own human capital should also have low correlation with your other investments.

For example, if you work for a high-tech company developing the next must-have computer gadget, website, or software program, don't put all your financial assets in the same high-tech sector as well. Why? These two investments — your human capital and your financial capital — would be highly correlated if they were invested in the same economic sector. In this case, your shortfall risk — the odds of regret — would be very high because, in all likelihood, if your human capital investment suffered, your financial capital would suffer as well.

In fact, there's a strong economic argument to be made

for investing part of your financial capital in your biggest competitor's stock. It, I would argue, will be negatively correlated with your human capital. If your company suffers, perhaps your competitor will succeed. In any event, you will have diversified. Yes, you may reduce some upside potential, but you will have definitely reduced your downside risk or probability of regret.

The same concept applies to those working in the financial sector, natural resources, or real estate. Diversify your investment capital so that it is not highly correlated with your human capital. If you are forced to hold a large portion of your wealth in your own company's stock — to align your incentives with those of your shareholders — then make sure you have some sort of downside protection.

But are mutual funds the way to go? Or should you pick these stocks yourself? Well, here is where we probed the question of risk-adjusted performance (Chapter 1). It's not enough to find a fund that makes money, or even to find one fund that did better than average. You have to assess the risk that fund was taking, and whether its performance compensated you appropriately for those risks.

To gain real confidence in the fund, its manager, or the company, you must convince yourself that this fund's performance cannot be attributed to chance alone. You must ask yourself: what are the odds that they were just lucky? Sure, there is no guarantee that, if skill was involved, they can continue to deliver positive performances. But if they were merely lucky, there is virtually no hope of persistence. If they have some skill, then at least you have a running chance. Be very selective and cautious. Few fund managers will admit that 60% to 70% of their colleagues do not beat the appropriate indices in the long run. Even fewer will tell you that you can invest in these same averages with no loads and fewer expenses, in the form of index funds, index baskets, and index-linked notes.

Of course, there is always the concern that one day, week, or month after you put your life savings into the mutual fund of your choice, the stock market will drop 20%. Isn't this the secret nightmare of every investor? So why not invest it slowly, using the technique known as dollar-cost averaging? In that way, you reason, you can avoid the horrendous consequences of picking the wrong time. Well, your intentions are admirable, but the implementation is faulty. As I argued in Chapter 2, dollar-cost averaging will not give you better odds. Lump-sum investing is superior, for the reasons described. This doesn't mean you shouldn't save regularly — that's a great idea. All I'm saying is that your volatility will be no further reduced by dollar-cost averaging than it would be by a simple asset allocation mix between equity and fixed-income securities.

But if lump-sum investing is the right way to go, if the motto is "invest now, when you have the money," then perhaps you should succumb to the temptation to borrow, in order to invest. Many people have done just that, remortgaging their homes and investing the proceeds in the (seemingly) never-faltering stock market.

Needless to say, no matter how you define risk, this strategy is risky. It only makes sense under very limited conditions, as I discussed in Chapter 6. Moreover, you have to distinguish between tax-deductible and non-tax-deductible debt, and make sure that you can afford the interest payments, without having to sell out at the worst possible time. Remember, the odds of losing money are magnified — in the early years — when you borrow.

But if equities are the place to be in the long run, does that mean there is absolutely no chance of regret — or at least of losing money — if I buy a diversified mutual fund and just hold it? Absolutely not!

The risk of shortfall and regret is always present; it may decline with the time horizon, but it will always be there.

In fact, this is one of the main selling features of death-protected mutual funds and variable annuities (Chapter 4) that offer some sort of money-back guarantees. The odds of regret are slim, but you still have to pay for the insurance, just as you would for your car, home, or even health insurance. The odds are low, but you still pay. Remember, the older you are, the more valuable that guarantee will be.

But at what age is it time to leave the party? After all, are your retirement years really a good time to be playing the stock market and taking (even minimal) shortfall risks? Well, again I would argue that the odds tend to favor a diversified portfolio of equity and fixed-income investments, even in your retirement years. With that in mind, I think people should defer the decision to annuitize as long as possible, because the odds are better if you leave your options open. As the computer simulations in Chapter 8 demonstrated, most people were better off waiting. This policy would apply to lump-sum settlements from pensions as well. Any action that you cannot reverse, such as reconverting your pension annuity to a lump sum, should be delayed as long as possible.

In fact, if I were designing my own retirement portfolio at age 65, I would probably invest 100% in the equities market. But immediately after the purchase, I would also buy some put options — funded by selling calls (Chapter 3) — to protect my downside in the event of a sharp correction. As time passed — and if markets moved up enough to completely fund my retirement — I would gradually sell off parts of these puts and calls. Otherwise, I would continue to roll over the options. To make this strategy work better and cost less, I would buy and sell so-called average rate options, as opposed to the standard puts and calls. The payoffs of average rate options, unlike standard options, are based on the average (as opposed to final) performance of the underlying security over the life of the option. So you end up making money if the average price was above (or below, depending on the type of option) a certain level, not just if the final price on the last day of trading was above (or below) a certain level. In a sense, you are insuring yourself against a long-term growth rate, as opposed to a market price on any particular day. This type of strategy is known as a contingent portfolio insurance scheme, and it is used by many professional institutional investors.

Does it sound too complicated for your personal finances?

Perhaps today, yes. But it won't 25 years from now. The future of personal finance is going to be much more complex. Think about it. Twenty-five years ago, the available personal financial options were pretty simple. After sinking a large portion of their capital into a house, investors could save for the future with stocks and bonds, a standard bank account, and maybe a mutual fund or two. Today, on the other hand, you are faced with a universe of products with exotic-sounding names like collateralized mortgage obligations, index funds, protective puts, protected mutual funds, real estate income trusts, STRIPS, Spiders, WEBS, deferred installment receipts, equity-linked notes, and even inflation-linked bonds. And I have probably missed a half-dozen other names and investment vehicles.

Who knows what the financial products of the future will look like? What financial innovations are we likely to see and what impact will they have on our financial lives?

Well, here is a light-hearted view of what your annual financial checkup might look like in the year 2025.

Your financial planner and registered nurse are scheduled to arrive in a few minutes to conduct the annual blood test. The test will determine whether there's been any change in your DNA's risk-aversion level.

Years ago, of course, regulators and compliance departments wanted investors to complete a "risk preference questionnaire" which guided advisers in assessing gen-

eral attitudes toward financial risk. Your risk profile would help them design an appropriate asset allocation, investment portfolio, and mutual fund selection. The legal form also protected them from liability in the unfortunate event that you lost an enormous amount of money — and wanted to sue them for negligence. But widespread fraud on the part of applicants, who constantly lied about their true attitudes toward risk, wreaked havoc on the integrity of the questionnaire process.

Fortunately, in the year 2007, Professors Hi and Lo, two bio-economists at Harvard University, working with a medical team from the National Institutes of Health, were able to isolate the gene that controls financial risk aversion. Although classical economists had postulated the gene's existence for years, there had been — until its discovery — no empirical evidence that humans were born with a unique and quantifiable attitude toward financial risk. Now, a simple blood test can determine the precise amount of financial risk that an investor is able and willing to tolerate. Inevitably, the Harvard researchers were jointly awarded the Nobel Prize in Economics and Medicine for this groundbreaking discovery.

The Hi & Lo risk-aversion metric is measured on a scale of 0 to 100. Higher numbers are associated with greater abilities to bear risk. Most Hi-Lo zeros exhibit a strong preference for keeping all their money in the form of gold coins buried in a steel case in their backyards; people in the 100 category seem to be completely invested in penny stocks of gold exploration companies in Indonesia.

Gene therapy soon followed, and many option, derivative, and hedge-fund traders were successfully treated to reduce their excessive risk-taking levels.

Federal regulators were quick to jump on the bandwagon, and the "know your client" forms were soon replaced with risk-aversion blood tests, which became affectionately known as "poke your client."

Well, maybe not exactly . . .

Last Words

As a professor, I'm always concerned that, no matter how much I hope for the contrary, my students will remember little — if anything — of my lectures a few months after the term ends. A buzzword here, maybe, or a slogan there, but most of the content will be gone. In a perhaps futile attempt to counteract this inevitable decay of knowledge, I always spend the semester's final lecture hour stressing the main points I want the class to remember — not just during the final exam (their principal priority), but years after I and the course are just blurred memories.

I make a series of statements to the effect of "If you run into me in a few years, I want you to tell me that you remember the following five things about this course . . ." This valiant effort seems to have had some effect. In fact, on those cheerful occasions when I do run into old students, I am always gratified by their attempts to remind me of that final lecture. But when it comes down to what exactly I had said, the conversation trails off. Oh, well. Perhaps the knowledge is hibernating in their subconscious, waiting to emerge one day, when they really need it, not just to impress me.

So what would I like you to remember, long after this book is collecting dust on your shelf?

Well, I could expound on how important it is to start saving for retirement at a young age. I could tell you that if you stop buying a cup of coffee every morning for the next 30 years — and save that money instead — you'll be able to buy a condo in Florida with the savings when you retire. I could talk about how much your child's education will cost in 20 years, or how many millions of dollars you'll need to retire in the year 2025. But my bet is that you've already heard these speeches from many other sources.

So I'd rather leave you with a simple, final thought. If there is one thing that's for certain, it's that the future isn't. Your financial future — and its success — depend on a variety of factors, most of which are outside your own and your financial adviser's control. Your financial future is random, uncertain, and unpredictable. What you can do, however, is become knowledgeable about the probabilities of regret associated with various courses of action, and then make decisions that minimize those same probabilities of regret.

I hope this book has given you a good indication of those factors that do — and those that do not — affect the probabilities of regret. If you regard every financial decision, from insurance purchases to monetary investments, as a form of medical surgery, you will constantly ask yourself: "Will this procedure give me the best odds? And if not, why am I doing it?"

Remember, calculate the odds. And then put them to work.

NOTES

CHAPTER 1

Your Investment Returns

This chapter draws on some of the mathematics that S. E. Posner (no relation to my colleague on this book) and I developed for our paper entitled "A theoretical investigation of randomized asset allocation strategies," published in the Spring 1998 issue of *Applied Mathematical Finance*. However, this topic is somewhat basic to modern investment theory, and was inspired by a paper I read in the Fall 1990 issue of the *Journal of Portfolio Management*, by A. J. Marcus. The author was trying to determine, statistically, whether the performance of Fidelity's Magellan fund could be explained by chance alone. After all, somebody has to win the race, and the winner of such a huge contest can be expected to earn phenomenal returns. His conclusion was that Magellan cannot be — surprise, surprise —

explained by chance. In fact, distinguishing randomness from skill — and the implicit ranking of risk-adjusted performance — has now become a sophisticated multi-million-dollar consulting industry. However, the basic technique and thinking can be applied to all funds, on the individual level as well. The more funds there are in a particular category, the less surprised I am to find one of them beating the index by an eye-popping 2,000 basis points. Also, please note that strictly speaking it is incorrect to interpret the probability of observing a particular data outcome, given the null hypothesis, as a probability that the null hypothesis is correct, given the data. The only way to obtain a posterior probability for the null hypothesis is to assume a probability of the observed event under the alternative, which is equally problematic. Also, from a technical point of view, please note that the numbers reported in Table 1.2 assumed normally distributed returns and excess returns — a strong assumption, given the sample properties. In plain English, we have made some strong assumptions about the nature of financial uncertainty. As with any model of reality, the data may not fit perfectly, but the general idea holds true. And the lesson is unfettered: "What are the odds the fund manager was lucky?" is the most important question to ask about any track record.

CHAPTER 2

Dollar-Cost Averaging

This chapter is based on a research paper written with S. E. Posner, entitled "Dollar-cost average options, Brownian bridges and behavioral finance." The paper examines the continuous-time distribution, and implications of dollar-cost averaging, in relation to its representation as an arithmetic option-pricing problem. It appears that if you compare dollar-cost averaging and lump-sum investing strategies when you *know*, or "condition on," the final value of the underlying stock, the expected return from DCA exceeds the return from LSI — and the higher the volatility of the stock, the greater is this effect. This is a behavioral explanation, but it does not justify dollar-cost averaging as a rational strategy. Indeed, the practice of dollar-cost averaging is widespread, and I am skeptical that this chapter will change many minds. Some additional articles that you may find interesting and helpful include "Lump-sum investing versus dollar-averaging," by M. S. Rozeff in the Winter 1994 issue of the *Journal of Portfolio Management*; "Nobody gains from dollar-cost averaging," by J. R. Knight and L. Mandell, in the 1991/1992 issue of *Financial Services Review*; "The fallacy of dollar-cost averaging," by S. Thorley in the Fall 1994 issue of the *Journal of Financial Practice and Education*; and "A behavioral framework for dollar cost averaging," by M. Statman in the Fall 1995 issue of the *Journal of Portfolio Management*. Most of these articles point out the inefficiency of dollar-cost averaging and the more effective alternatives for reducing risk. I do not question the psychological importance of a systematic savings plan; it's the investment strategy that bothers me, as it does many others.

CHAPTER 3

Home-Cooked Portfolio Insurance

This chapter is loosely based on my paper with S. Kim published in the Fall 1997 issue of *Financial Services Review*. In that paper we decompose some basic index-linked structures into their respective option components. Specifically, we show how to create an index-linked structure using standard options. For an advanced treatment of financial options — and how they can be used to create portfolio insurance and downside protection — see "the bible" on option pricing: J. C. Hull's *Options, Futures and Other Derivatives* (fourth edition), published by Prentice Hall in 1999.

CHAPTER 4

Variable Annuities

This chapter is based on my research paper with S. E. Posner, entitled "The Titanic option: Valuation of the guaranteed minimum death benefit in variable annuities and death protected mutual funds." Feel free to download the paper for the technical details and underlying assumptions. The main message of the paper, namely, that the value of the death benefit is between 1 and 13 basis points, has generated quite a lot of publicity and controversy. The paper has been quoted in, and I have been interviewed by, *Business Week*, *Barron's*, *The Washington Post*, *Money* magazine, and a dozen other regional papers. I have also been contacted by consumer advocacy groups, regulators, and insurance companies, and have even been asked to testify in class action lawsuits launched against companies who sell variable annuities in qualified plans. Therefore, it is *extremely* important that I emphasize my fundamental position that there is nothing intrinsically wrong with variable annuities. (In fact, some of my best friends have variable annuities.) The best example is TIAA-CREF, which sells a variable annuity with a mortality and expense charge of only 7–10 basis points. In my opinion, that is a fair price for the guarantee, and their product is an excellent investment *if*: you have used up your room in all other qualified investment shelters; you plan to invest only in fixed-income products; and you believe your marginal tax rate will be much lower during retirement — since the variable annuity is not an efficient use of qualified plan assets. For additional information, please see my paper "Mortality derivatives and the option to annuitize" (with D. S. Promislow) and "Options by installments with application to protected funds" (with T. S. Salisbury). They are posted on my website, **www.milevsky.com.**

CHAPTER 5

Diversification

This chapter is based on a paper I presented at the 1998 meeting of the Academy of Financial Services in Chicago, entitled "Space-time diversification: Which dimension is better?" The basic idea — which was inspired by the groundbreaking work of A. D. Roy in the 1950s — is to compute the shortfall probability for various holding periods and time horizons. Both dimensions reduce risk, but the marginal benefit depends on the current size and holding period of your portfolio.

CHAPTER 6

Investing on Margin

This chapter is not based on any academic paper or active research work. It is a simple and straightforward look at the concept of borrowing to invest. The probabilities are computed by evaluating the lognormal distribution at the required quantiles.

CHAPTER 7

Asset Allocation After Retirement

This chapter is based on a series of very popular and award-winning research papers I have written with K. Ho and C. Robinson on the optimal trade-off between risk and return during retirement. Other excellent sources of information are the papers "Self-annuitization and ruin in retirement," by M. A. Milevsky and C. Robinson, which is forthcoming in *The North American Actuarial Journal*; "Asset allocation via the conditional first exit time," by M. A. Milevsky, K. Ho, and C. Robinson, in the July 1997 issue of the *Review of Quantitative Finance and Accounting*; and "How to avoid outliving your money," by M. A. Milevsky, K. Ho, and C. Robinson, in the Fall 1994 issue of the *Canadian Investment Review*. I have been asked to present the results of this research to thousands of investors and retirees, as well as brokers and financial planners. In fact, we have recently developed some software that locates optimal portfolios by controlling the probability of starvation at higher ages. I would, however, like to discourage a formulaic application of the optimal retirement allocation — searching for the one that gives the lowest starvation odds — without examining the many other relevant factors, including but not limited to simply reducing levels of consumption.

CHAPTER 8

Life Annuities

This chapter is based on a paper I published in the September 1998 issue of *The Journal of Risk and Insurance*, entitled "To annuitize or not to annuitize?" The paper, although somewhat technical and mathematically cumbersome, presents a series of computer simulations that examine the odds of beating the mortality-adjusted rate of return from a life annuity. The results contained in that paper, however, are reported conditional on survival (this was forced upon me by an unyielding reviewer), so they uniformly overestimate what I call the true odds of shortfall. In any event, the idea is the same. As per the technicalities, the continuous-time mortality rates were taken from a Gompertz distribution that was fitted to the 1996 SOA Individual Annuity Mortality table with dynamic projections. Please note the distinction between expectation-of-life and median life. The median life numbers in the chapter were obtained by computing the 50% point on the above-mentioned Gompertz distribution. In any event, and with the usual caveats, I believe people should keep their options open and defer annuitization as long as possible. Although finance theory has yet to price the irreversibility premium in a fixed-life annuity, it certainly has value. I should emphasize, once more, the importance of fees when deciding whether or not to defer annuitization. If you are considering a low-cost fixed immediate annuity, and the implied interest rate the insurer is using in its pricing is very close to "market rates," then by all means go ahead and annuitize. Indeed, the TIAA-CREF immediate annuity (in their qualified plan) is another example of an excellent product offering extremely low fees. Finally, in a recent paper of mine with N. Charupat and H. Tuenter, entitled "The market for fixed and variable life annuities and its effect on risk-taking behavior," we document the substantial benefits that can be obtained from purchasing variable as opposed to fixed-rate annuities at retirement.

CHAPTER 9

No Regrets

The question of how to define financial risk is the subject of an ongoing debate among finance academics and practitioners. The most vocal and prominent opponent to time diversification and shortfall as a measure of risk is the Nobel laureate, Professor Paul Samuelson, at MIT. In fact, in a private letter to me, dated 18 March 1997, he wrote:

> Moshe . . . I regard the 1952 Roy shortfall criterion as a determiner of stochastic portfolio decision making, to

> be arbitrary and unappealing. Life is not a vanity-game duel; that is for the sports pages. What counts for me are the different money outcomes that chance will deal out for each choice-criterion I try to maximize, and how I will feel about each algebraic increment of money outcome. . . . Take my cold water with many grains of salt. Max Planck said: "Science progresses funeral by funeral."

Please see my working paper entitled "In defense of shortfall as a rational measure of risk" for a detailed description of this debate.

The following books are excellent for further reading on risk, regret, and the stock market.

Peter Bernstein. *Against the Gods: The Remarkable Story of Risk*. Toronto: John Wiley and Sons, 1996.

Ron Dembo and Andrew Freeman. *Seeing Tomorrow: Weighing Financial Risk in Everyday Life*. Toronto: McClelland and Stewart, Inc., 1998.

Burton G. Malkiel. *A Random Walk Down Wall Street*. New York: W.W. Norton and Company, 1996.

Jeremy J. Siegel. *Stock for the Long Run: A Guide to Selecting Markets for Long-Term Growth*. Concord, ON: Irwin Professional Publishing, 1994.

INDEX

adverse selection, 146–47, 149–50
adviser, financial. *See* consultants, investment
age
  and annuitization, 141–42, 150–51
  and death benefit fees, 79–81
American Greetings Corp., 89–90
American Stock Exchange, 17, 60–61
annuities, 141–42, 147, 161. *See also* life annuities; self-annuitization; variable annuities
  immediate, 68, 73–74, 140
annuity death benefit. *See under* benefits
appreciation rights, 62
asset allocation, 42–43, 118–19, 174. *See also* retirement
asset classes. *See specific types of assets*

balanced funds, 27
basis points, 27
baskets, index, 173
benefits
  annuitization, 73–74
  death, 70–73, 79–81, 83
  tax, 67–70, 78
bequests, 162
bond funds, 27
bonds, 27, 104, 158, 167
  government, 29, 84
  zero-coupon, 52–55, 58
borrowing. *See* leverage
brokerage accounts, 52
brokerage fees, 59–60, 84
Buffett, Warren, 15–16, 25–26

call options, 55
  at-the-money, 56, 58–59
  out-of-the-money, 56–57, 58, 59, 62
capital gains tax. *See under* taxes
caps
  death benefit, 71, 72
  growth, 51, 59, 62

cash-value insurance. *See* life insurance
causality. *See* chance; skill, investment
CD. *See* certificate of deposit
Centers for Disease Control. *See* mortality tables
certificate of deposit (CD), 7, 29, 49–50
chance, 15, 19–22
clustering, 26, 28
commissions, 84
commodities, 58, 104
commutability, 161
computer programs, 104. *See also* Monte Carlo simulations
consultants
  investment, 52, 63, 104, 136
  performance, 23
consumer advocates, 23
consumer price index, 121
correlation, 94–96
  and diversification, 96–99, 172
  and human capital, 172–73
  and time horizon, 100–102
correlation coefficient, 89, 101–2
costs
  lost opportunity, 51
  transaction (*see* transaction costs)
Country Baskets, 17

data mining, 46
DCA. *See* dollar-cost averaging
death
  benefits at, 70–73, 79–83
  and taxes, 69
debt. *See* leverage
deposit, certificate of, 7, 29, 49–50
Depository Receipts, S&P 500. *See* Spiders
deposits
  bank, 7
  term, 167, 168
diversification, 4. *See also* correlation; risk
  international, 89, 94, 172
  and investment choice, 89–90, 104, 105, 175
  and movement of investments, 88–89, 102–3, 172
  pros and cons of, 90, 99
  and risk, 92–94, 99, 102
  success factors in, 99, 102
  and time horizon, 100–103
  trade-offs of, 90–91
  types of, 94
  and volatility, 40, 41
dividends
  and index-linked notes, 51
  rights to, 62
  as source of income, 124
  from Spiders, 61, 63
  and taxes, 69
dollar-cost averaging, 31, 174
  advantages of, 38
  alternatives to, 34–37, 40, 41, 44
  definition of, 32
  disadvantages of, 38, 40, 43
  new versions of, 46
  reverse, 121
  and variability, 42–44
  and volatility, 36, 40
downside protection
  with index-linked notes (ILN), 51–52
  with zero-coupon bonds, 52–55
dual uncertainty model, 127–28

Efficient Market Hypothesis, 18
equities
  and annuities, 158
  and diversification, 40, 102, 103–4, 175
  investment in, 63, 118, 170–71, 174
  rate of return on, 132
equity funds, 12–13. *See also* mutual funds
  and risk, 167–68, 170
  and volatility, 27, 40, 41, 166
equity put options, 61–62
equity risk premium, 132
estate planning, 162
Europe, stock market in, 94–96
event conditioning, 144–45
expense ratios, 29, 74–78

fees. *See also* commissions; transaction costs
  brokerage, 59–60
  insurance, 73, 79

management, 61, 65–66, 70, 74
variable annuity, 81–82, 84–85
financial adviser. *See* consultants, investment
Financial Engines, 135
fixed-income investments, 94, 118, 174, 175
fixed-term annuities, 147
floor. *See* benefits, death
fluctuation. *See* volatility
foreign currencies, investment in, 58
401(k). *See* plans, qualified
403(b). *See* plans, qualified
fund managers. *See* mutual funds
fund regulators, 23
funds, 26–27, 29. *See also specific types of funds*

gains
capital, 61, 63, 68–69, 115
realized, 67, 83
unrealized, 67–68
global economy, 89, 94, 95–96
Gold Standard Inc., 89–90
growth caps, 51, 59, 62
guaranteed annuitization rate, 74, 83
guarantees, money-back, 114, 175

health. *See also* mortality tables
and annuitization, 142, 150
and wealth, 146
holding period, 5–6

ILN. *See* index-linked notes
income taxes. *See* taxes
indexes, stock. *See* stock indexes
index funds, 17, 29, 76, 83–84, 173
indexing, 121
index-linked notes (ILN), 49, 50–51, 62, 173
as downside protection, 51–52, 114
replicating, 52, 58, 60–62
upside potential of, 58
Individual Retirement Accounts (IRA), 66. *See also* plans, qualified
inflation
evolution of, 8, 120–21
reducing risk from, 94, 161
insurance. *See also* benefits, death
charges for, 70, 79–81
life, 81, 147, 151–52
portfolio, 176
variable annuities as, 72–73
insurance companies. *See also* variable annuities
fee calculations by, 79, 84
and life annuities, 147
interest. *See also* leverage
affordability of, 108, 114–15
as source of income, 124
and taxes, 115, 174
interest rates, 8, 50, 91
and annuities, 142, 159–60, 161–62
and leverage, 110, 174
international equity funds, 26
investments, 4–6, 17, 29, 63, 94. *See also specific types of investments;* annuities; diversification
active versus passive, 17, 29
in the competition, 172–73
long-term, 39, 40–41, 134
picking, 15–17, 29
and retirement planning, 127, 160
short-term, 169–70
IRA, 66. *See also* plans, qualified
IRR, 158–59

Japan, 94

Keynes, John Maynard, 87

leverage, 107–8, 174
downside of, 109, 112–14, 171–72
upside of, 108, 109–12
liability, tax. *See* taxes
life annuities, 140, 147, 148
alternatives to, 151
cautions about, 159–62
deferred purchase of, 150–51, 153–56, 159, 175
and taxes, 69
life insurance, 81, 147, 151–52
life span, 145–46. *See also* longevity; mortality tables
median, 142–44

liquidity, 29, 61, 94, 161
loans. *See* leverage
longevity. *See also* life span
  insurance against, 147
  patterns of, 131, 142–46
longevity risk, 141
lost opportunity cost, 51
LSI. *See* lump-sum investing
luck. *See* chance
lump-sum investing (LSI), 34–35, 39
  compared to dollar-cost averaging, 34–37, 174
Lynch, Peter, 15–16, 26, 87

managers, mutual fund. *See under* mutual funds
margins. *See also* leverage
  outperformance, 25–27, 29
market timing, 46
market trends, 8, 45, 46–47, 91–92
metals, precious, 58, 104
Microsoft Corp., 89–90
money-back guarantees, 114
money market investments, 29, 134, 168
  liquidity of, 94
  managers of, 26
  rate of return on, 131
  and risk, 7
  as source of income, 124
  and volatility, 27, 40, 41
Monte Carlo simulations, 8–9
  of deferred purchase of annuities, 154–55
  of leverage, 110–13
  of retirement planning, 129–31, 134–35
  of variable annuities, 66, 78–79
Morningstar Inc., 12, 66, 75
mortality. *See under* risk
mortality tables, 129, 131, 149
mutual funds. *See also* expense ratios; fees
  benefits of, 14, 105
  compared with bank accounts, 42
  compared with stock indexes, 13, 16–17, 23, 25
  compared with variable annuities, 65–67, 82–83
  evaluating, 11–14, 23–24, 29–30, 173
  managers of, 15, 16–17, 24, 29–30
  performance records of, 11–14, 23–24
  and retirement planning, 66, 175
  returns on, 41–43
  and risk, 7, 173
  and taxes, 67, 69
  transaction costs of, 13, 16, 132
  and variability, 42–44
  and volatility, 26–27

National Center for Health Statistics, 142–43, 149
needs
  analysis of, 118–19, 121
  reducing, 127
Needs-to-Wealth ratio, 123
net asset value (NAV), 61
New York Stock Exchange, 17
notes. *See also* certificate of deposit
  short-term, 49

odds. *See also* Monte Carlo simulations
  conditional, 144–45
  of regret, 39
option pricing theory, 163
options
  annuitization, 73–74
  average rate, 175–76
  call, 55–59
  put, 57, 82
outliving your money, 124–29, 132–35, 140–41
outperformance margins, 25–27, 29

pension funds, 23
pensions, 175. *See also* plans, pension; Social Security
  creating, 139–40
  private, 118, 120, 121
  and tax regulations, 140
performance, investment, 11–14. *See also* mutual funds, evaluating
  adjusting for risk, 26, 173
  reporting on, 23

performance consultants, 23
performance penalty, 45
period-certain annuities, 147
permanent life insurance. *See* life insurance
planner, financial. *See* consultants, investment
plans, pension
  non-qualified, 140
  qualified, 54, 66, 83, 85, 120, 140, 152–53, 162
  tax-sheltered, 54
portfolio. *See also* diversification
  balancing, 104, 158, 175
  insurance for, 176
premiums
  contract, 70
  option, 55, 57
  return of, 71–72, 79–80
price-paths, 36–37, 45
Probability of Regret, 5–6, 154–55, 167, 174–75
profitability, 159
programs, computer, 104. *See also* Monte Carlo simulations
prospectuses, 23
protection, downside. *See* downside protection
put options, 57, 61–63, 82, 114

qualified plan. *See* plans, qualified

ratchet provision. *See* benefits, death
rates of return, 29, 131–32, 157
  on index-linked notes, 51
  internal (IRR), 158–59
real annuities, 161
real estate investment, 94, 104
regret, probability of. *See* Probability of Regret
regulators, fund, 23
reports, shareholder, 23
research, economic, 44–45
retirement. *See also* pensions; plans, pension
  asset allocation for, 118–20, 175
  and income taxes, 122–23
  and mutual funds, 66
  outliving your money in, 124–29, 132–35, 140–41
  planning for, 178–79
  and variable annuities, 69
returns, 40–43, 132, 134
rights, 62
risk, 91–93, 105, 132. *See also* leverage; speculation; volatility
  adjusting performance for, 26
  management of, 7, 8
  mortality, 81, 150
  reducing, 99, 102, 114
  of the sum, 100
  systematic, 91
  over time, 7, 167, 170
  tolerance for, 47–48, 104, 176–77
  unique, 91, 92, 94, 105
  unsystematic, 91
roll-up. *See* benefits, death

sales charges, 70
savings, forced. *See* dollar-cost averaging
savings bonds. *See* bonds
self-annuitization, 140–41, 153, 157–58
service charges, 74–75
sex differences, impact of
  on death benefit fees, 79–81
  on longevity, 144–45
  on retirement planning, 125–29, 134–35
shareholder reports, 23
Sharpe, William, 135
short-term investments, 39, 131, 134, 168. *See also* bond funds
  compared with long-term, 169–70
skill, investment, 15–16
  versus chance, 15, 19–22, 24
Social Security, 118, 120
Society of Actuaries, 83
speculation, 170–72
Spiders, 17, 60–63
S&P 500 index, 13, 16, 58, 130. *See also* Spiders
standard of living, 118–19
Standard & Poor's, 60. *See also* S&P 500 index
starvation probability. *See* outliving your money
step-up. *See* benefits, death

stock indexes, 58. *See also specific indexes;* index-linked notes
  compared to mutual funds, 13, 16–17, 23, 25, 29
stock markets, 94–95, 165–66. *See also specific stock markets;* market trends; trading
stocks
  compared to other investments, 7, 105
  and short-term money, 39
strike price, 55–56, 57
STRIPS, 52–55, 58
sum of the risk, 100

tax brackets, 66, 68–69, 122–23
taxes
  and bonds, 54, 84
  and capital gains, 61, 63, 68–69, 115
  at death, 69
  deferred, 68, 83–84
  and interest payments, 115
  and pensions, 140
  and retirement, 122–23
  and variable annuities, 68–69, 70, 73, 83
tax penalties, 69
tax shelters, 54, 66, 68, 70
  withdrawals from, 121, 122
T-bills. *See* treasury bills
term deposits, 167, 168
term insurance. *See* life insurance
TIAA-CREF, 66, 75
time horizon, 7
  and correlation, 100–102
  and investment, 5–6, 42
  and risk, 167, 168, 170
timing, market, 46
trading
  data on, 46
  of Spiders, 60–61
  strategies for, 46–47
transaction costs, 70, 74–75, 84. *See also* fees
  and options, 59–60
  role of in mutual funds, 13, 16, 132
treasury bills, 131–32, 166, 167

underwriting, insurance, 73
United States, stock market in, 94–96
U.S. Decennial mortality tables, 129, 131
U.S. equities. *See* equities

Vanguard, 66, 76
variability of investment returns, 42–44
variable annuities (VA), 140, 175
  advantages of, 66, 83
  compared with life insurance, 81
  compared with mutual funds, 65–67, 68, 82–83
  conversion into life annuity of, 69, 73–74
  disadvantages of, 68–70
  expense ratios of, 75
  fees for, 81–82, 84–85
  low-cost, 66
  payout options of, 68, 70–73
  and taxes, 68–69, 70, 73, 83
volatility, 165–66. *See also specific types of investments*
  and clustering, 26, 28
  and death benefits, 81–82
  of different types of funds, 26–27
  and dollar-cost averaging, 36, 40
  effects of asset allocation on, 42–43
  and long-term return, 40–41, 132, 134
  reduction of, 36, 40, 42
  and time horizon, 42

WEBS, 17
Wilshire 5000 index, 13
withdrawals, systematic, 121, 122

zero-coupon bonds, 52–55, 58

ABOUT THE AUTHOR

Moshe Arye Milevsky is a tenured finance professor at the Schulich School of Business at York University in Toronto, Canada, and is a principal at the financial engineering consulting company Quantingale M.C. He has a Ph.D. in Finance (1996), an M.A. in Mathematics and Statistics (1992), and a B.A. in Mathematics and Physics (1990).

The focus of his teaching, research, and consulting work is on the interplay between investment management, personal finance, and insurance. In addition to teaching Ph.D., MBA, and BBA courses, he gives many public seminars and has developed innovative training programs for individual investors, financial planners, and brokers all across North America. He is also the author of the bestselling book *Money Logic: Financial Strategies for the Smart Investor*, which was published in Canada in 1999.

Moshe has received numerous awards and research